REWIND

REWIND

A Caregiver's Neurodiverse Life, Frame by Frame

James S. Harper

Content Warning:

This memoir contains suicidal thoughts and acts. Reader discretion is advised. Throughout this memoir, I explore many facets of life, including death and moments of profound despair. At my lowest point, I journaled my thoughts and reflections, which became a wake-up call and a catalyst for my determination not to let it consume me.

Cover Art

The front cover features the "Rewind" crank of a 35mm SLR film camera — a symbol of looking back and revisiting memories.

The back cover displays the film transport surface of a 35mm SLR film camera, emphasizing the theme of reflection and captured moments.

Having pursued photography from high school graduation until age 30+, I chose this imagery to reflect the book's theme of revisiting life's moments, frame by frame.

Paperback ISBN: 979-8-9924834-0-6

First Edition

Visit the book's companion web site at WhatAboutLife65.wordpress.com. James S. Harper earned his degree in Psychology from Kent State University.

To my son,
I hope this book imparts some life lessons in case
I'm not able to share them with you in person

Author's Note:
Some names and identifying details have been changed to respect privacy. However, the events and experiences recounted in this memoir are true to the best of my recollection.

Visit the book's companion web site at:
WhatAboutLife65.wordpress.com.

Table of Contents

James S. Harper

Preface

There's a strange clarity that comes from looking back—like peering into a fogged mirror, where images slowly sharpen. For much of my life, I watched from the sidelines, wondering why I felt different—more like a visitor in my own story than a participant. The world often felt unpredictable and just out of reach, and I spent years collecting fragments of myself along the way. Each step—wrestling with language, struggling to decipher social cues, or quietly battling dyslexia—felt like trying to solve a puzzle without ever seeing the picture on the box.

Dyslexia was a roadblock I learned to work around, though not without scars. Words, sentences—even thoughts—refused to arrange themselves neatly in my mind. Writing them down felt like untangling a knotted thread—pull in one direction, and another strand tightened. Over time, I adapted by seeing the world visually, finding comfort in images and moments that made sense without explanation. But even as I excelled at photography, my way of framing the world felt different, as though certain pieces of human interaction remained just beyond my grasp.

It wasn't until much later—far later than I might have imagined—that I found a name for these lifelong mysteries. Autism. The discovery was like placing the first corner piece of a jigsaw puzzle, a revelation that redefined my experiences and gave meaning to years of feeling like an outsider looking in.

This story follows my journey as I gathered these clues—the moments when autism offered me a unique perspective, when dyslexia forced me to adapt, and when life itself tested my resolve. It's a story of searching for myself while moving forward, even when the path was unclear, and holding on to hope when direction felt lost.

And yet, it all began to make sense on a cold winter night as I stepped into my mother's home—a place steeped in memories, holding answers I wasn't sure I wanted to find.

Winter Gloom

As my evening flight descended into the winter gloom of Cleveland, I couldn't shake the weight of the task ahead. Just five months earlier, on Labor Day weekend, I had returned to Cleveland to pick up Mom from a nearby assisted living facility—a stopgap solution until my sister could arrange a room for her near Boston. We stopped by the house for one last look before heading east.

While I was there with Mom, the attorney called.

"Jim, your brothers have alerted me that they called the police"

Of course, they did.

"They told them you're moving their mom out of state without their approval."

My grip tightened. It was typical. They waited until the last minute to interfere—when the decision had already been made, when I was already standing there, bags packed, with Mom looking at me like she wasn't sure where she was.

"Do I, as Mom's POA and son, have the legal right to move her?" I kept my voice level.

There was a pause. The attorney exhaled. "Jim, just hurry."

I didn't argue. They weren't the ones here. My brothers lived hundreds of miles away, an eight-hour drive at best. They had opinions, but they weren't the ones making the daily calls, scheduling the care, or dealing with the doctor's warnings.

Amidst this tension, it became our final visit together in this house. We packed what little remained—essential clothes, a few cherished mementos from the last thirty years. The rest would be packed and moved in a few weeks.

I looked at Mom, sitting in the corner across from the front door with Megan, her toy poodle, in her lap. She gazed around, eyes darting over the room as if trying to place where she was. Her fingers stroked Megan's fur, slow and uncertain. I watched as her brow furrowed, her mouth slightly open, as if she were searching for something just beyond reach. My heart grew heavy, knowing the reality.

"You'll come back, Mom," I assured her, even though we both knew better.

I should have been straightforward with her, but part of me couldn't face that truth. Perhaps I was protecting her, or maybe I was protecting myself. I clung to a sliver of hope that somehow, things would be different—that maybe there would be another chance for a more organized transition.

But reality spoke louder than wishful thinking. In the end, neither of us could escape what was coming. The move to an assisted living facility near my sister's home was the best option for Mom, despite the ache it left in my heart. With no family in Cleveland and my brothers miles away, relying solely on the kindness of friends was unsustainable.

It was late, the clock nearing midnight, when I reached the front door. Holding the storm door open with my body, I inserted the key, turned it, and pressed down on the latch. As I stepped inside, the still air was heavy with memories, the silence amplifying her absence. A chill crept over me.

The first-floor rug still bore the shadows of furniture removed. It felt as if life had been put on pause. Megan wasn't there to greet me. Only the echoes of ghosts whispering stories of years gone by. Mom had lived here alone for the past fifteen years, meticulously redecorating each room as each child left the nest.

In October, we had the movers pack up and ship most of the furniture to Boston for her new apartment at the assisted living facility.

Over the past few years, during my holiday visits, I had noticed the gradual accumulation of clutter in the front bedroom. I simply saw it as disarray, unaware that it was a telltale sign of her dementia. Living far away in Denver, I felt helpless in the face of her struggles.

The echoes of her battles reverberated through the empty rooms—shouts, pleas, the sharp edge of panic.

Memories of that July night clawed their way back—the night that nearly took her.

Someone had seen to it that her Valium prescription was cut off abruptly. No tapering, no medical guidance—just an abrupt stop. The withdrawal hit hard. She lost all sense of time, of reality, of herself. She screamed at the walls, at people who weren't there. She ran outside in her bedclothes, barefoot on the pavement.

My sister called, her voice tight with concern. "Jim, the neighbor called. She said Mom was outside in her bedclothes—disoriented and confused. I contacted the attorney to get help and to look into a better living arrangement."

Mrs. Daniels, a kind neighbor who had known Mom for thirty years, had seen her outside, confused. She led her back inside, kept her calm, and called for help. No family was in town—just strangers. The first responders pieced together what had happened.

This was the breaking point. Mom had fought against having anyone in her home, resented the idea of supervision, but the doctor's orders weren't suggestions anymore. The next step wasn't a choice.

Earlier that summer, I had returned to Cleveland on short notice for a neurologist consultation. I wasn't expecting what came next. After speaking with her, the nurse didn't hesitate.

"She needs institutionalization," she said bluntly.

I was taken aback. Institutionalization?

Mom sat beside me, stiff. Her lips parted slightly, as if about to protest, but then she pressed them into a tight, thin line. Her eyes burned with quiet defiance. She clenched her purse a little tighter in her lap, fingers curled white against the leather. This was the same woman who had spent years helping me through my own struggles. The woman who had fought for me when I was drowning in words I couldn't read. Now, she was the one being told she could no longer care for herself.

I couldn't simply stand by and allow some nurse to dictate Mom's fate. Before leaving at the end of those turbulent four days in June, I arranged for a visiting nurse to attend to her daily, preparing her lunch, ensuring she took her medications. It wasn't just a recommendation from the doctor but a mandate, under the looming threat of neglect charges if I failed to provide the necessary care.

I adjusted the thermostat to a cozy 72 degrees before ascending the stairs. Despite the familiarity of the house during my breaks at boarding school, it felt foreign to me now. The bedroom I once claimed as my own was transformed into Mom's office, a silent testament to the passage of time.

The front bedroom, once my sister's, was a mess of garbage bags stuff full of papers and my task for tomorrow.

In contrast, my younger brother's old room, the smallest in the house, remained relatively uncluttered. Yet, its cramped space and odd angles always unnerved me, perhaps due to its proximity to the bathroom or the way the roof intersected one wall.

Crawling into the cold bed felt more like an intrusion than a retreat, lacking the comfort of a generic hotel room. Fatigue and the looming tasks ahead dulled the discomfort of being alone in the silent house.

Morning brought a renewed sense of purpose. Rising at 7:00, I ventured out for breakfast, returning armed with extra-large, heavy-duty garbage bags. The hazy daylight filtered through the windows, casting a somber glow over the empty rooms. I contemplated turning on the radio for company but hesitated, as if honoring the absence that permeated the space, memories now lost to Mom's advancing dementia.

Sorting through the piles of bags Mom had amassed in the front bedroom became my mission for the day. Decades of mail, receipts, bank statements, and tax forms lay in disarray, most of it destined for the trash. Hours passed as I meticulously sifted through each item, determined not to discard anything of importance.

Beneath a pile of old tax forms, a flash of blue caught my eye. I tugged it free, fingers brushing the satiny fabric. I knew right away what it was—my first ribbon from Red Raider Camp.

The days prior to my 21st birthday, I had purged my collection of ribbons and other items, deeming them relics of childhood, a bygone era. But here it was. She had saved it. I turned it over, tracing the edges.

The paper tag on the back was still firm, untouched by time. A lump rose in my throat. I hadn't realized she cared that much, a poignant reminder of the bond between a mother and her child, or maybe, I had just never let myself believe it.

Hmm. Red Raider...

Red Raider Camp

Wow, Red Raider Camp . . .

"A one! A two! A three! Give me a yell, give me a yell, give me a big substantial yell, and when we yell, we yell like this and this is what we yell! Gazimme, cazamme, gazzam, hip hip, hooray, hip hip, hooray, yay Red Raider!"
I'm Red Raider born and
Red Raider bred,
And when I die, I'll be Red Raider dead,
Rah-rah-rah, Rah-rah, Red Raider, Raider,
Rah-rah, Red Raider, Raider, Rah-rah, Red Raider Camp!
RAH! RAH!

Every time the bus entered Red Raider Camp and started up the steep, rutty dirt driveway, we erupted into shouts and sang the camp's jingle. It felt like the start of a TV show—something I knew a lot about. But this—this was the most fantastic show ever. Everyone on the bus had a starring role, and I was in it.

Their voices filled the air, each laugh and burst of excitement taking the place of any jumping that might have occurred on solid ground. I watched them, absorbing every expression—like studying a scene. Soon, I found my part. Camp was my home. I belonged, even if only on the fringe of the deeper games being played.

She saved this ribbon. My first ribbon and a first-place blue ribbon, no less.

Red Raider Camp, hmm. That was such a magical place. Our bus driver was named Wow. Maybe those were his initials, but to us campers, he was just Wow. He was a tobacco-chewing, short and round man who waddled as he walked. I had never seen anyone like him in my five or seven years of life. My world was filled with teachers, doctors, and adults in suits and ties. But Wow was different—a real character in my eyes. Every now and then, as we drove to camp, he would crank open the bus door and spit. I always kept an eye on that door, wary of what might come through it.

The camp counselors had strange names too—Moose, PW, Poncho, The Nurse, and Fox. They seemed like they had stepped out of Saturday morning cartoons, like they belonged to some secret world where only kids and oddball grown-ups were allowed. Maybe all camps were like this, but to me, it was pure magic.

When I was five, my parents started sending me to summer day camp. My two brothers and sister also went, but not for as long as I did. Those days marked the beginning of an eight-year journey, one of the few splurges my parents indulged in for us. I think they were just happy to get us out of the house during the summer.

At camp, I didn't have to struggle with letters that flipped backwards or upside down, or pretend I wasn't lost in the middle of a paragraph. I could run, climb, and build fires without worrying about the jumble of words waiting for me in books. Without camp, I probably would have just watched more TV, retreating further into that safe, familiar world.

I remember the first day of camp vividly. It was early morning when Mom walked me to the corner of our block to wait for the camp bus. The night before, we had found a discarded cardboard box at the grocery store—big enough to hold everything I needed, yet sturdy enough not to fall apart under the weight of my camp gear.

"Let's make sure you have everything," she said, kneeling beside me as we packed. She reached in and adjusted the towel, folding it tighter. "Swimsuit?"

I nodded.

She tapped the folded fabric. "Jacket?"

"Yeah."

She picked up the blanket, smoothing it before placing it back on top. "This should keep you warm at rest time," she murmured, almost to herself.

I watched her tuck the corners of everything, securing it as if she were sending me off on something bigger than a summer camp. I didn't know what camp was or what to expect. The uncertainty gnawed at me, a mix of excitement and apprehension. I just knew that tomorrow, I'd be getting on a bus—and wherever it took me, I'd have this box.

Mom waited with me at the end of our street to make sure I was picked up by the camp bus. Soon, I spotted a yellow-orange school bus with black front fenders chugging down the street. It looked older than the ones at Boulevard Elementary, well-worn from years of use. The red letters along its side—Red Raider Camp—felt like a ticket to another world.

I needn't have been apprehensive. The Jumper, the lead counselor on the bus, checked off my name on the roster, and we continued our route, picking up more campers. The ride to camp buzzed with laughter, songs, and excitement.

After the last camper boarded, the Jumper began leading the bus in songs. I had no idea what the words were, but many seemed easy enough to follow. I just thought it was so great being with other kids full of fun and joy. The singing and laughter made the bus feel like its own little bubble of reality as it rumbled down the road toward camp.

"*John Jacob Jingleheimer Schmidt! His name is my name too—*

Whenever we go out,

The people always shout, . . ."

The entire bus shook with singing voices

"*There goes John Jacob Jingleheimer Schmidt.*

Dah dah dah dah, dah dah dah"

Kids sang loud, their voices spilling into the summer air.

"*There's a hole in the bucket, dear Liza, dear Liza—*"

The Jumper, shouted over the singing, "Quiet Hill!"

The singing stopped. Mid-chorus. No one spoke. The only sound was the low rumble of the bus slowing as we descended into the Chagrin River Valley. The usual chatter disappeared, replaced by the grinding of gears and the rustling of tree branches against the open windows. The scent of damp earth filled the air.

As the valley swallowed us, the voices vanished, as if someone had turned the volume knob down. I glanced around. No one exchanged looks or whispered explanations. It just... was. I held my breath, waiting for some sign to reveal the secret.

At the bottom of the hill, as if on cue, everyone picked up where we had left off.

"There's a hole in the bucket, dear Liza,
There's a hole."

The voices swelled again, the spell broken.

We crossed the bridge singing . . .

" Zip-pi-di-doo-da, zip-pi-di-day
My, oh my, what a wonderful day—"

"Quiet Hill!"

The bus began the steep climb out of the valley, groaning as Wow downshifted, the engine straining. A gust of wind swept through the windows, carrying the echoes of the chorus up the hill. Then, just as we crested the top, the voices returned, as if nothing had happened.

"Plenty of sunshine headin' my way . . ."

I didn't learn the reason for Quiet Hill that first day, but over the summer, I understood. It was part respect, part superstition, part necessity—a way of slipping between two worlds: the one we left behind and the one we were about to enter.

Red Raider Camp waited just ahead.

At the beginning of each summer camp session, the Red Raider Knight sat tall on his horse at the edge of the pine trees lining the entrance, his silhouette backlit by the morning sun. His red cape draped over his shoulders, unmoving in the still summer air, his metal helmet gleaming. As the bus turned into the camp's steep driveway, we erupted in our camp cheer.

It always struck me as odd—on the valley hills, we had to be quiet. But here? Here, we were anything but silent.

The bus made its usual left turn onto the dirt road and paused. The engine idled, gears grinding as the driver readied for the climb. That pause was our signal. We sat up straighter, bracing for it. Then, as the bus lurched forward, we unleashed it all at once:

"A ONE! A TWO! A THREE! . . ."

The shout burst from us like a collective roar, bouncing off the trees. The knight never flinched. He just sat there, watching us, as if standing guard over a place that belonged to another time.

The camp was divided into upper and lower camps. Upper and lower not only described the location—upper camp being further from the buses, but also the age of the campers. We were assigned to groups by age, all named after Native American tribes. In the nineteen-sixties, there wasn't the concern about political correctness that we have today.

That was a good thing, because I learned many Native American tribe names from camp, like Blackhawk, Sioux, Mohegan, Hopi, Cherokee, to name a few. Sadly, with the exception of Western movies on TV, if the camp hadn't used these names, I might never have been exposed to that culture at all.

Red Raider Camp provided a daily schedule packed with activities: swimming, crafts, sports, hiking, and outdoor skills like making a fire and pitching a tent. In those years, the tents were old army surplus canvas tents with no floor, just a simple inverted V. I liked most of the camp activities—with one exception. First-period swimming.

Northeastern Ohio summers were humid, but mornings were often cool. Dampness clung to everything, from the leaves in the trees to our cardboard boxes on the floor of the Adirondack shelter. We'd hang our swimsuits outside after each lesson, but by morning, they were never dry. At best, they were damp. More often than not, they were cold and soggy to our touch as we pulled them on.

Imagine shedding your warm, dry clothes and stepping into a wet bathing suit that had been hanging in the woods all night. Yowwie. Even at that age, talk about shrinkage—and there wasn't much to shrink.

With our damp suits brushing against our skin, we made the walk to the pool, towels draped around our shoulders for whatever warmth they could offer. Some kids shuffled in flip-flops, but most of us walked sockless in hiking shoes, our legs bare to the morning air. The dirt path often just a drip from being muddy as we walked. By the time we reached the pool, we were already shivering.

Sally, the swim instructor, stood at the edge of the water, wrapped in her robe. Bone-dry.

"Okay, boys, jump in."

She said it like it was nothing. I eyed the pool, even the water looked cold with its blueish still water reflecting the painted blue of the pool. I hesitated.

"Why don't you take off that robe and join us?" I muttered under my breath. But there was no arguing. We had to get in.

Some kids crept toward the edge, dipping their toes, sucking in sharp breaths. Others went for it—leaping in, gasping, their arms flailing as the shock hit them. I knew better than to delay the inevitable.

I jumped—

WHOOSH.

The cold knocked the air from my lungs. My skin felt like it had been slapped. I kicked hard, pushing to the surface, gasping as my head broke through.

"Start bobbing!" Sally called out.

I bounced up and down in the water, my teeth chattering. They always said the best way to handle the cold was to keep moving. I don't remember it getting warmer, but at least it became tolerable.

Sometimes, when it was particularly cold, an instructor would build a small campfire next to the pool. On those days, I endured the lesson by keeping my eyes locked on the flickering flames, willing the time to pass faster.

Oddly, I liked those mornings. The chill, the smoke curling through the air, the way the sunlight filtered through the branches—it was miserable and beautiful all at once.

Red Raider Camp was big on horseback riding. A factory for little horseback riders, one instructor had called it.

I vividly remember my first time riding a horse. It was a particularly hot day, the air thick with the smell of dust, manure, and straw. We sat on worn wooden bleachers along the edge of the outdoor riding ring, waiting our turn. The sun had baked the dirt, and every so often, a horse would flick its tail, swatting away flies. Their hooves clopped lazily in the dust, stirring up clouds that drifted toward us.

One of the instructors stood in front of the bleacher, his hands on his hips.

"Alright, listen up. No sudden moves, no shouting. You scare the horse, you scare yourself."

I watched the older kids go first, climbing into the saddles with what looked like practiced ease. I wasn't so sure about this. The only animals I had ever been close to were dogs—and they didn't stand five feet tall.

"You're up," a counselor said, nodding toward me.

I walked forward, heart pounding. The horse they had assigned me stood still, his large brown eyes watching as I hesitated.

"Put your left foot in the stirrup," the counselor instructed.

I lifted my foot, trying to reach the stirrup, but it barely made it past the horse's knee.

"Hold on," I heard behind me, "I'll give you a boost up" as the instructor came over.

Once up I barely could straddle the leather saddle. The seat felt unfamiliar beneath me; my balance unsteady.

"Now, sit up straight. Hold the reins gently—like you're holding a bird. Not too loose, not too tight."

Like a bird? I thought. I never held a bird nor had I held a horse's reins.

I mimicked what I saw the others doing, adjusting my grip, shifting in the saddle.

Then the horse moved.

A single step.

I froze.

Oh no. This was a mistake. I'm going to fall off. It's a long way down.

"Relax," a counselor said.

I swallowed. Relax? I was perched on an animal the size of a small car. But I forced myself to loosen my grip. Slowly, I let go of the front of the saddle, sitting upright.

Something changed.

The fear faded—not entirely, but enough. The longer I stayed on, the more I began to trust the rhythm, the sway of the horse's movements.

After a few laps around the ring, my nerves had settled. I found myself looking around, taking in the new view from this height. The sounds of camp faded—the shouts, the rustling trees, the scrape of hooves in the dirt. There was just the horse beneath me, the leather reins in my hands, the rise and fall of each step like a heartbeat I could finally match.

For the first time, it was just me and the horse, moving together.

At the end of the summer, when they handed out awards, I was stunned to hear my name. A white-painted horseshoe with "M.I.R."—Most Improved Rider—etched into it was given to me.

I turned it over in my hands, tracing the letters. Me? Most Improved?

I hadn't thought of myself as a rider before that moment. But maybe, just maybe, I might become one.

My interest in riding grew, and soon Mom started coming to watch me on Saturdays. After one of my lessons, she lingered by the fence, watching the others ride while I brushed my horse down. That's when I overheard her talking to the instructor.

"He really seems to enjoy this," she said to the instructor, almost as if realizing it for the first time.

The instructor nodded. "He's doing well. He's got a good seat—natural balance."

Mom turned to me. "Would you like to keep riding in the winter?"

I froze, mid-brush. I hadn't expected that.

"Really?"

"Why not?" she said with a shrug. "It's better than you sitting inside watching TV all weekend."

I didn't care about her reason. In that moment, all I knew was that I wanted to say yes.

School wasn't fun, but camp had been. Riding meant I could keep that part of camp alive, even during the winter.

When I wasn't riding, I was in front of the TV.

The flickering screen filled the room, casting blue-tinted shadows on the walls. I knew every theme song, every commercial jingle. When a character spoke, I didn't need to mouth the words—I already knew them. Their world played out before me, familiar and predictable, a place I could watch but never step into.

I didn't have many activities I enjoyed other than my paper route. I liked delivering the papers early in the mornings before the sun was up—the quiet streets, the sense of independence. But collecting the money was a different story.

It wasn't about getting paid—it was about knocking on strangers' doors, standing awkwardly as they fished for change or, worse, having to make small talk. Some houses were huge, their front doors towering over me, making me feel too small, too out of place. Once I had enough money to cover my paper bill, I stopped collecting altogether.

Of course, this didn't sit well with my customers, especially when I showed up weeks later asking for payment. Funny how my habit of enjoying the work more than the pay would come back to haunt me later when I needed to make a living.

So I began riding on Saturdays, surrounded by other kids who also enjoyed it. Riding was different from other activities I had tried, like baseball or football.

I had never been good at team sports. I was always the last one picked, and my coordination didn't help. Swinging a bat, kicking a ball—how did you know when to swing? Some kids seemed to just feel it, but for me, it was a guessing game. If I made contact with the ball, it was pure luck.

Catching, hitting, throwing—none of it clicked. In baseball and football, the ball always seemed a step ahead of me, as if it had its own plan I couldn't quite follow. But riding? Riding had a rhythm. I could feel the horse beneath me, the steady sway, the way my body synced without hesitation. No second-guessing. Just motion. And I could do that.

The best part was the instructions. With horseback riding, there was always an instructor nearby—guiding, correcting, showing us exactly what to do. I wished more of life worked that way.

I felt good on horseback. For once, I wasn't struggling to keep up. I wasn't out of sync. The other kids in the lesson talked to me like I belonged, like I was just another rider—not the kid who didn't get the joke or couldn't keep up in gym class.

Red Raider Camp had been a bright spot in my life, a place where I could belong and achieve something. It had been an escape from the difficulties of my world, a fleeting taste of what it felt like to connect with others, even if I didn't fully understand it then.

Perhaps that's why my mom saved this ribbon—because, in her own way, she knew how much those moments meant. They were the bright spots in a challenging childhood. Moments where I could be a young boy lost in the magic of summer camp—if only for a little while.

* * *

Reluctantly, I placed the blue ribbon in the trash pile. I knew all too well how nostalgia could suffocate—pulling me into memories long gone, stealing time I couldn't afford to lose that weekend. There was no room for lingering in the past.

At twenty, I had gone through everything I had collected up to that point, discarding most of it—objects that tied me to my youth. I would soon be turning twenty-one, a full-fledged adult. But as I packed my most cherished belongings into my VW Fastback, I found comfort in one small token—the M.I.R. horseshoe. I had preserved it, the first award I had ever received. Its weight in my hands had once given me an unexpected sense of achievement, a feeling I rarely experienced.

This small object became an anchor, steadying me as I let go of the past. I have it to this day. What struck me, even now, was that Mom had saved this ribbon. Out of everything, twenty-five years earlier, she had quietly chosen this one to keep.

I grabbed the two large trash bags I had filled and made my way downstairs to the garage. The house had never truly been home. Mom bought it after the divorce, around the time I was entering ninth grade. The move from Brentwood marked the end of an era.

I was sleeping over at a friend's when she called and told me to come home.

When I walked through the door, she was waiting. Without a word, she led me upstairs, away from the noise of the house, into her bedroom. She sat down on the chaise lounge, patted the space beside her, and took a slow breath, smoothing her skirt as if ironing out the words before they came.

Her voice was soft, but the weight of what she was about to say settled between us, heavy and inevitable.

"Sweety... your father and I... we're getting a divorce."

Mom's words lingered, waiting for a reaction I didn't have. The room felt too quiet, as if expecting a gasp or tears that wouldn't come. I traced the pattern in the carpet with my eyes, searching for something steady, something certain.

The distance between them had been there for years—I had seen it long before they made it official. But deep down, I still wished they had stayed together as my parents, just more civilized.

Outside that room, life would go on. The fights would stop. The house would feel different. But sitting there, listening to Mom say the words out loud, I only felt the space between us—the pause where she waited for me to react.

I gave her a small nod. "Okay."

The late-night fights had been relentless, their voices echoing through the floors, seeping into my bedroom no matter how hard I tried to block them out. I wasn't the only one looking for an escape.

Skipper, our dog, was, too. When the yelling got bad, I'd hear him at my door—scratching, pushing it open if I hadn't latched it all the way. He'd slip inside, escaping the voices downstairs, then rest his head on my bed as if he knew I needed the company. I like to think we were comforting each other. Dogs have that sense.

Skipper wasn't just my nighttime refuge—he was my buddy, the one who tagged along on my paper route in the early mornings. While I went house to house, he trotted alongside me, tail wagging, sometimes getting ahead, as if he already knew the route.

During junior high, I became more aware of music—not just as background noise, but as something that spoke to me. The songs of the sixties carried messages of peace, love, and change. Their lyrics became lifelines.

It was in high school when I was helping with the Sunday service, I learned that the Byrds' "Turn! Turn! Turn!" wasn't just a song—it came from Ecclesiastes 3. *"To everything there is a season, and a time to every purpose under heaven."* I stumbled upon the passage in the Bible, and for the first time, I saw how lyrics could hold deeper meaning—how songs weren't just something you heard, but something you felt.

But no song resonated more than Three Dog Night's "Out in the Country." I played it often, letting the words settle inside me:

Before the breathing air is gone
Before the sun is just a bright spot in the nighttime
Out where the rivers like to run
I stand alone and take back something worth remembering.

It reminded me of Red Raider Camp. The woods. The river running beside the trails. The feeling of freedom—away from the noise, the conflict, the confusion of home. Camp had always been my refuge. A place where I could breathe. A place where I could escape the harsh realities of life—and, for a little while, just exist in a world that felt lighter.

As I walked through the empty first floor, it felt devoid of any memories that might have made it feel like home. This house, which had been home to my younger brother and sister during their high school years, no longer held the personal significance it once did.

My time at boarding school, where the focus was on addressing my reading difficulties, had created a distance from my childhood ties in Cleveland, the city where I was born. Returning home on breaks had always felt surreal, like stepping into a place I was supposed to belong but no longer did.

Now, standing in the house, preparing it for sale, that feeling hadn't changed. Without the comforting presence of camp, I had often felt adrift, and the years had only deepened that sensation. It was strange, this constant feeling of being a visitor—not just in my old home, but throughout much of my life.

My Brother and I

Walking through the kitchen toward the garage, I passed by the stairs leading to the basement. I dropped off the trash bags, but before heading back upstairs, I felt an urge to confront the mess below.

The basement was worse than I had imagined. It was filled with boxes and furniture, still unsorted and long forgotten, pressed in from every side, leaving only a narrow footpath down the stairs to the laundry area. The air was thick, tinged with dust and the faint musty scent of time.

I paused at the bottom of the stairs, surveying the clutter, the weight of it all settling onto my shoulders. How was I going to clean all of this out? What was I supposed to do with it all?

I'd seen houses in Denver where a massive 40-foot industrial dumpster was parked in the driveway. The piles were unsettling—framed pictures stacked like forgotten memories, clothing draped over broken furniture, a potted plant long dried out and brittle. A life scraped into a dustpan, waiting to be hauled away. How sad it was that some lives ended in a pile of discarded belongings.

Disgusted, I turned to head back upstairs, but something pulled me toward the old darkroom. I quickly opened the door, stepping into the small, dark space my younger brother and I had built under the stairs. It was my first darkroom, where I had spent countless hours, especially before I left town at twenty. The memories came flooding back.

By fifth grade, I was getting too old for day camp, so I got to go to overnight camp. Overnight camp exposed me to many new experiences and a few life lessons. One of the most vivid memories was from The Beehive, the arts and craft building at camp. It consisted of one large room with several cupboards where craft materials were kept.

That year, a counselor had a passion for photography. He transformed an unused, chicken-wired cage in one corner into a makeshift darkroom. One day, I was invited along with a few others to watch him make a photograph. Four of us squeezed into the tiny darkroom. Along the wall was the enlarger and a set of developing trays, each with a pair of bamboo tongs. The first thing I noticed was the sharp, vinegar-like smell of the stop-bath solution.

The counselor announced that he was going to make a print, and we needed to shut the door because any light would ruin the light-sensitive paper. The room was dimly lit by a single orange light. After a few seconds, my eyes adjusted to the darkness. We watched as he placed a negative in the enlarger, then reached for the pack of paper, placing a blank sheet on the easel. He set the timer for ten seconds and turned it on.

We saw the negative image light up the paper. The light went out, but the paper remained white. Odd, I thought—there was no picture. Had something gone wrong?

Then, the paper was placed in the developing tray. I leaned in, wide-eyed making sure I did not miss anything. The counselor tilted the tray back and forth ever so slightly to keep fresh developer washing over the piece of photopaper.

Slow as a sunrise, a ghostly outline appeared, then darkened, the details sharpening like fog lifting from a valley. Magical! That first experience with photography at camp was the spark, but it was in this very darkroom under the stairs that my passion truly took hold.

My younger brother and I grew closer during those summer months. He was eighteen months younger, and while most of the year we were two years apart, his summer birthday brought us within just a year of each other. Somehow, that subtle shift made us feel closer. Maybe it was our ages or just the carefree spirit of summer that made the difference seem less important. Whatever the reason, we did a lot together.

He was always the first to strike up a conversation, to dive headfirst into an adventure. But when the day wound down, it was just the two of us. No crowd, no group—just him, just me, just the summer stretching wide before us.

That summer, when I was twenty, we went to a parachute spot out in the country. I didn't have the money for a jump—and truthfully, I was fine with that. But my younger brother needed to test his courage; he had a bit of an adrenaline junkie streak.

It was fascinating to watch how they prepared. I stood by as he practiced by jumping off a four-foot-high platform, simulating the force of a parachute landing. He'd land on both feet, then roll to his side, absorbing the impact. He came back from the actual jump all pumped up.

"Jim! You gotta try this!" He ran up, eyes wild with excitement. "Come on—just once!"

I shook my head. "How much?"

He grinned. "Too much." He patted his pockets. "Yeah… I really don't have the money either." He nudged my shoulder. "Let's ride."

So we rode our motorcycles through the country roads, making stops along the way. I took a few photos, capturing those moments.

That Labor Day, we stood side by side, heads tilted skyward, the roar of jet engines vibrating through our chests. He leaned forward, eyes locked on the tight formations, restless, charged.

"That's what freefall feels like," he muttered, his fingers twitching as if he could already feel the air rushing past. I just watched, content to keep my feet on solid ground.

As I prepared to leave Cleveland that fall, I had one last photography project in mind. I came across a flyer at the Art Institute for Cleveland's New Organization for the Visual Arts (NOVA) annual photography contest, and though I'd never entered one before, I was eager to give it a shot. With my plans to move already in motion and knowing I wouldn't be around for the exhibition; I figured I had nothing to lose by submitting my work.

I sifted through my negatives but couldn't find anything that felt right. Then, perhaps inspired by Jerry Uelsmann's multiple image prints, two images from that summer with my brother caught my eye. One was of us stopped along a country road after his skydiving adventure, and the other was a tight formation of fighter jets from the air show. The skies in both photos were eerily similar.

An idea struck me: I could blend the jets into the sky of the motorcycle shot. It would create an odd but intriguing image of fighter jets looming over a peaceful country road. I titled the photograph "My Brother & I." Despite its flaws, I submitted it.

In early October, just weeks before my departure, I received a letter from NOVA. My photograph had been accepted for exhibition at a well-known art gallery in December. The news was thrilling, adding to my growing excitement for life after the disappointments of college. I wouldn't realize how exclusive the NOVA show was until I was nearly fifteen hundred miles away.

Now, standing in the basement, only a stepstool occupied the space where I once stood, printing that photograph. I ran my fingers along the shelf, tracing the shallow notch where my enlarger had once rested. A thin layer of dust clung to my fingers. The air lacked the sharp, vinegar bite of the stop-bath, yet the memory of it lingered. The darkroom, stripped bare, felt like a hollow shell—a ghost of the past, missing only the trays, the enlarger… and me. It had been so long ago, yet the echoes remained, faint but persistent. I pushed the plywood door shut, sealing it behind me, and headed upstairs.

Baby Folder

I kept working through each bag in the front bedroom, piece by piece, slowly making headway. The silence in the house was heavy, almost oppressive, leaving me alone with my thoughts. Why hadn't I brought a radio? Something to kill the silence, something to drown out the constant churn of my own mind. Each piece of paper I picked up felt like a grain of sand slipping through the hourglass of Mom's life down to the final grains.

My own life wasn't going so well either. My marriage had ended— or rather, it was in the final throes, but it was close enough. Thank goodness we didn't have children. And work… well, work wasn't much better.

I wasn't done, but I had made my way through each bag in the front bedroom when I noticed the daylight was fading, and I realized I hadn't even stopped for lunch. Hunger gnawed at me, pulling me out of my daze.

Tying up the filled garbage bags, I carried them down to the garage before heading out for a bite of dinner. After grabbing a quick bite to eat, I returned to the house, now dimly lit in the early evening shadows.

I moved on to Mom's office—my old bedroom. As I sorted through the clutter, I came across folders she had kept on each of her four children. Like many parents, she had saved mementos from our early years. I quickly skimmed through my sibling's folders until I found mine, saving it for last, as if bracing myself for what I might find.

I was curious about my past, particularly anything that might shed light on my reading difficulties, my dyslexia. I recalled Mom once mentioning that doctors had considered the possibility of autism but had concluded that I was too highly functioning to fit the definition.

In the mid-1960s, the concept of an Autism spectrum hadn't yet emerged. Dyslexia became the label for my struggles with reading and spelling. My social challenges were attributed to low self-esteem and the social isolation that dyslexia supposedly caused.

Inside the folder with my name on it, I found a treasure trove of memories: my baby book, old school report cards, gift cards I had made for Mom, and class photos from elementary school.

The baby book, titled *Our Baby's First Seven Years*, immediately drew me in. On the first page, it noted that my grandparents had given it to my parents, and it contained the precise details of my birth: day, time, location, all neatly inscribed. At the bottom, it had the signatures of my dad, mom, the delivering doctor, and nurse. The next few pages held hospital records, a tiny blue beaded bracelet with my last name spelled out, and newspaper clippings from various birth announcements.

One announcement even noted that my parents had briefly considered naming me Warren, with the nickname "Woody." I shook my head, grateful they hadn't gone through with that. The book also contained locks of my hair, baby photos, and medical records, but what I was most interested in were the little notes that could shed light on who I was in those early years.

I had no idea if any of the milestones I read about happened at the "normal" time, but at 3 months old, I was standing while leaning on Mom during bath time. At 6 months, I was crawling around the house, and by 13 months, I was walking on my own. It made me smile to read that at 5 months, I splashed so hard during baths that I soaked the bedroom floor. Mom had kindly documented the chaos with humor, noting how much I loved it.

One comment under the heading "Bladder Control" caught my attention. I was 2 years and 8 months old when she wrote, *"It seemed like Jimmy would never 'train,' but suddenly, almost overnight, he became completely bowel and bladder trained ... His control seemed to start when he saw me putting his younger brother on the toilet."*

I found this fascinating because I've always learned best through visual observation. Once I see something done, I can usually replicate it with ease. When assembling anything, I only need to see the finished product or a diagram, and from there, I can piece everything together without much trouble. It's always been that way for me.

Then I saw a note from when I was 2 years and 9 months, almost 3 years old. Mom had written, *"Jimmy is talking very little ... many of his words are not clear to others. However, he understands everything said to him perfectly, and he makes himself understood to us by pointing and taking us to what he wants."*

It struck me how kind and gentle her description was, softening the edges of what might have worried another parent. Mothers have a way of seeing the best in their children, even when others might not.

Now, I realize that my delayed speech was an early sign of what would later be understood as part of being on the autism spectrum, along with dyslexia. While my words struggled to form, my mind was already working differently, processing everything around me with a deep, quiet understanding. Mom's note captured that unspoken complexity, her words a subtle shield from the harsher labels others might have placed on me.

Elementary School

I liked going to the school's library—or any library. I was fascinated by the rows of bookshelves, each packed full, their spines forming a continuous plane—a pattern of curved edges lining the shelves. To an elementary school kid, the library felt enormous. Bookcases lined each wall, and a row of windows bathed the space in natural light. At the very top, about seven feet up—but to me, it could have been seven stories—were signs labeled *Fiction, Non-Fiction, Art,* and a few other categories that looked official and important.

There were rules in the library, and they had to be followed. No loud talking, only whispers. Respect the books. Turn the pages with care, starting at the top corner of the right-hand page and slowly turning it over, making sure not to crease or bend it. The librarian reinforced these rules with a quiet but firm presence, watching over us like a guardian of knowledge.

I liked the small round step-stool that hovered just above the floor. When you slid it across the floor, it sounded like a muffled metal drum, then landed with a decisive *clunk* when you stepped on it, locking into place.

And then there was the card catalog—a magnificent wooden structure, polished to a fine smoothness, each drawer gliding out effortlessly. Inside, hundreds of cards held the key to every book in the library, meticulously typed with the title, author, topic, and location on the shelves. Running my fingers over the cards, I marveled at the hidden world they contained, an index to knowledge beyond my reach.

The library was pristine, perfectly organized. Every book held words, and those words told stories or contained important facts. They were all waiting for me. But life had other plans.

I enjoyed school, especially in the early years. First grade was filled with the excitement of learning to read. I remember the thrill of recognizing short, one-syllable words in two- to four-word sentences. *'See Spot. See Spot run. Run, Spot, run.'* I didn't sound out the words—I repeated what I had heard, matching the letters to the way they had been spoken. I'd read it aloud, adding a bit of flair as if I were performing: *'SEE Spot. See Spot RUN. RUN, Spot, RUN.'* It felt like a significant accomplishment, and I was proud of myself.

Second grade was even more significant because that's when we really began to read. The sentences grew longer, some with five or six words, and even a few had two to four syllables. Reading was becoming more challenging, but I was still excited about it. Then, one day early in the school year, everything started to unravel. It's a moment that remains vivid in my memory.

During reading time, the teacher divided our class into four groups to give us more individualized attention. I was placed with what I felt were the brighter kids—Brian, Betsy, Maggie, and John. We took turns reading pages from our *Dick and Jane* book. At first, it was thrilling. The pages were familiar, similar to what we had read the previous year.

But then, on my second turn, I hit a wall. The words grew longer, the sentences stretched out, and suddenly, I was struggling. I tried to recall the words as I had done before, but they weren't familiar. I didn't know how to break them down. The letters on the page didn't tell me how the words sounded—I was supposed to just *know*.

With the teacher's help and some gentle prompting from my friends, I managed to get through it, but it got harder each time. I couldn't keep up.

As my classmates continued to read with ease, I felt myself fading into the background, like I was disappearing. Inside, I was screaming, *Help me! I don't understand why I can't read like you. Help!* But no one could hear the battle raging in my head.

When I was young, no one explained why I struggled. I didn't know that schools had moved away from phonics, that kids were now expected to memorize whole words instead of sounding them out. Maybe if phonics had still been taught, I would have learned sooner that certain letter combinations weren't meant to be read separately. Maybe I wouldn't have felt so lost.

By third grade, reading and spelling had become sources of embarrassment. I'd stumble over words, mispronounce them, or freeze when I encountered something unfamiliar. I vividly remember a session with my after-school tutor. We came across the word *together*. I started with "tog," then got lost trying to piece together the rest. I saw "the" in the middle and got even more confused.

The tutor was patient. She suggested I break the word down. "What's the first part?" she asked, covering up the rest of the word with her fingers.

"To," I replied.

"Good. Now, what does this say?" she asked, revealing just the middle three letters.

"That's easy. 'Get,'" I said.

"And the last part?"

"Her."

"Great. Now say the word."

"To get her," I said, puzzled.

"Yes. Say it again, but faster."

"To get her."

"That's right."

I was still confused. To get her? That doesn't make sense in the sentence.

"Say it again, faster."

"To get her."

Finally, she sighed and said slowly, "To get her, together."

"Oh," I thought, "you blend the 't h.' It's not 'get her'; it's 'gether.'" I felt a bit frustrated, thinking she could have just told me to blend the 't h' right from the start. That small piece of knowledge which phonics could have provided would have made reading so much easier. Instead, I spent years stumbling through words, trying to memorize them rather than understanding how they were constructed.

The other kids seemed to move and interact in a world I couldn't quite grasp, as if they spoke a language I could hear but not understand. I accepted early on that I didn't fit in. Conversations slipped past me, and when laughter erupted or someone made a joke, I was usually a beat too late to respond.

It wasn't that I didn't know what was happening—often, I did. But by the time I processed the words, the moment had already passed, leaving me feeling like an outsider, always observing but rarely participating.

One day, during the second half of the school year, I was pulled aside at the start of reading period.

"Jim, please follow me to the hallway," the teacher said.

My mind and heart raced. Had I done something wrong? Was she going to send me to the principal's office? That's what happened when a teacher asked you to step out of the classroom. As I entered the hallway, another woman stood waiting.

"This is Mrs. Morris," my teacher said.

"Hi, Jim. Nice to meet you," she greeted me with a warm smile.

"She's here to help you with reading," my teacher explained, her voice even — matter-of-fact, not unkind, but firm enough that I knew this was not optional.

I felt a mix of relief and dread. On one hand, it was nice to escape the classroom, away from the prying eyes of my friends who found reading so easy. But on the other hand, I knew this meant I was different.

I liked Mrs. Morris's kind and gentle demeanor. For the rest of my elementary years, she would call me out of class, and we would head downstairs to the basement. Walking the hallways at that time of day, when they were mostly empty, gave me an entirely new perspective on the school.

It felt like being backstage at a play, seeing the set from an angle most of my classmates never would. The familiar spaces — classrooms, lockers, bulletin boards — looked different when they weren't filled with students. It was as if I had stepped outside of the regular rhythm of school, existing in a quieter, parallel version of it.

On our way to the basement, we passed the teachers' break room, which always smelled strongly of coffee. But what really intrigued me was the boiler room.

The janitor was often leaning against the huge door, which seemed impossibly thick — at least two or three inches — standing eight feet high and six feet wide. I know now it was just a boiler room, but as a fourth grader, it felt like a dark cave hiding some mechanical monster. The pipes and boiler cast eerie shadows, and every so often, strange sounds rumbled from behind the door. I would steal glances past the janitor, half expecting to see glowing eyes peering back at me from the dark abyss.

Mrs. Morris gave me many tests and reading exercises. Some of them seemed downright ridiculous — like one machine that flashed strings of letters and numbers, and I had to recall what I saw. Memory retention, I guess. The projector would flash the strings, and I had to repeat them, with the flash interval shortening from seconds to fractions of a second. I had no idea how this was supposed to help me read, but I was surprised at how much I could remember in those fleeting moments.

There were perks to being tutored that no other kid had. In sixth grade, I got to see the very first video camera the school system acquired. The teachers were unpacking a brand-new Sony black-and-white video camera and recorder, and Mrs. Morris asked if I wanted to see it. Boy, did I ever!

They were struggling to figure out how to connect everything. I quickly glanced at the pictures in the instructions, then at the cables, and had it all running in no time—to their amazement. I thought they were just playing dumb to make me feel better, but looking back, I realize they genuinely had no idea how to use it.

I liked leaving class for tutoring, especially if it got me out of a boring lesson. But each time I stepped out of that room, it felt like I was being slowly pulled away from the world of the other kids, like the door closing behind me was also closing off a part of their lives from mine.

When my classmates asked where I went, I hesitated. How do you explain a place no one else goes? I could have said 'reading help,' but the words felt like an admission, not an answer. Instead, I shrugged, letting the question pass, leaving them to imagine something more exciting than the truth. It only deepened the divide between me and the other kids.

I'd jump into a conversation, trying to match their rhythm, but my words landed just offbeat—like a song slightly out of sync. Faces turned toward me, some amused, some puzzled, before the moment rolled on without me. I'd make mistakes that felt so stupid, writing "techer" instead of "teacher" or "Bulvard Skool" instead of Boulevard School on the blackboard.

One day, I was at the blackboard, thinking I was doing okay, when I heard a soft "Pssst." A cute girl in class pointed to what I had written, her expression a mix of shock and pity.

My heart sank. I didn't know what I'd done wrong. I scanned the alphabet painted above the blackboard, trying to figure out if I had mixed up a letter again. My brain scrambled for an answer, but the harder I thought, the blanker my mind became.

And then came the slow, creeping heat of embarrassment—the way my body felt too big and clumsy, my hands too damp to grip the chalk properly. My face flushed, beads of sweat forming on my forehead, as if I were losing control of myself.

The chalk kept slipping, mixing with the sweat on my palms to form a thin, chalky paste. I wiped my hands on my pants, but all I left behind was a smeared white handprint on my leg.

I felt like I was shrinking, as if the classroom and everyone in it were pulling away from me, leaving me smaller and smaller, disappearing into the background.

"Oh, good grief!"

Reading was supposed to be fun, but for me, it was like trying to climb a mountain in the dark. I loved books, but they were a struggle. Each summer, we had to read a book, and I'd only manage to finish a few.

But I remember one summer when I read "Dorp Dead". It was about an orphan who struggled with reading too, taken in by a cruel man who tormented him. In the end, the boy found the courage to scratch "Dorp Dead" (Drop Dead) on the man's door. That story stuck with me, I guess I saw a bit of myself in that boy, fighting to find my voice in a world that didn't make sense.

By fourth grade, the isolation of dyslexia had fully set in. When November rolled around, I turned ten. I was proud of that two-digit number, but it didn't change the fact that no matter what I did, I always felt a step removed.

"Class, I've got exciting news," the teacher began. "See this large blackboard? As a class, we will draw a world map. I got us new colored chalk." I noticed that even the chalk carried a subtle, quiet promise of creativity soon to fill the vast 12-by-4-foot canvas.

Instantly there was chatter among the kids. Even I was excited. Finally, a chance to work with the other kids, to be part of something bigger than just me.

She divided the class into groups of four to five students. I was eager and waiting for her to call my name. Instead, she walked over to me.

"Jim, I have a special item for you to make—the compass rose," as she pointed to the lower right corner of the blackboard.

My heart sank as I saw the blank corner—a stark contrast to the bustling groups forming elsewhere. While the room buzzed with laughter and whispered plans, I found myself staring at a tiny, forgotten patch, far removed from the center of the action. What? No North America with five other kids, no Asia or Europe—just me, in the corner drawing a compass rose. Alone.

I poured all my effort into it, the lines were precise, the letters crisp and it turned out great. But it was just me, alone in the corner, while everyone else collaborated on the continents.

"Good grief."

Learning cursive was another hurdle. At first, I was thrilled— writing like an adult, connecting the letters in that flowing script. But soon enough, the excitement faded. The words got longer, the letters harder to connect, and I had to focus so much on spelling that the flow of cursive became impossible.

Handwriting was never just about putting letters on a page; it was a slow, exhausting process. My mind had to first recognize each letter— distinguishing between b, d, p, q, t, f, h, n, a, o —a task that wasn't automatic.

Then, I had to take that mental image, translate it into the correct hand movement, and carefully make the letter—all while making sure I spelled the word correctly. Every step required conscious effort, each letter a separate battle.

Printing was no less involved, but at least I didn't have the added complexity of figuring out how the letters connected while also struggling to form them. In cursive, my brain had to juggle not just the shape of each letter, but how it flowed into the next, an extra layer of processing that overwhelmed me.

There was no fluid motion, no ease, just an uphill struggle to make my thoughts visible. I eventually gave up and went back to printing — childish, maybe, but at least it was something I could manage. Yet another way I was set apart, excluded from what the others seemed to do so effortlessly.

The real kicker that year was the fake Beatles performance. It was talent day, and while I had no talent to show off, Steve, Bret, Tom, and Mark had the whole class mesmerized. They pushed four desks together to make a stage and lip-synced to a Beatles song, using metal cigar tubes as fake microphones with string as cords dangling off them.

The girls went wild, swooning over their every move. I couldn't understand why this silly act had them so mesmerized. It was just four guys pretending to be famous musicians. But the girls screamed like they were at a real concert, and the rest of the class cheered like they were watching magic.

I didn't get it. I never would. I felt even more invisible, just another kid fading into the background while everyone else shined.

"Good grief, Charlie Brown!"

Mom always said I was a "happy child." Maybe she was right. I remember noticing kids who seemed overly happy, almost oblivious to the world around them, lost in their own bubble. Perhaps, I was like that. Compared to some of my classmates, I suppose I was happy.

I saw sadness too—like in Nancy, a girl from my third-grade class. She carried an invisible weight, something more than her size. I sensed the teasing, the whispers that followed her, and wondered if her life at home was hard, too.

Then there was Johnny, a boy from my neighborhood who tried hard to be the tough guy, masking his own troubles with cruelty. I seemed to slip past his radar. Maybe it was because I was too wrapped up in my own world to hear his insults, or maybe he saw no sport in targeting someone who was already an outsider.

I had a knack for avoiding the harshness of others, a skill that served me well through life. It began when I was very young. During recess, I was often one of the last kids picked for sports, a ritual that reminded me of my place on the sidelines. With my wimpy stature, I wasn't a viable pick. My reading was already a daily failure. So, I found other ways to spend recess—not playing, but observing.

I saw the girls as something different, a group defined by their similarities. They played games that didn't rely on strength but on rhythm, precision, and companionship—hopscotch, jacks, jump rope. Girls, it seemed, started as a collective, bound by shared interests and unspoken rules, until one eventually stepped forward to stand apart.

The boys, by contrast, were defined by competition. They demanded individuality from the start—who could run the fastest, throw the farthest, or climb the highest. Their teams were built on rivalry first, then loyalty, forged through common goals and brute strength.

Where was there room for someone like me? I wasn't built for their games, and I didn't have the instincts for their unspoken challenges. But sometimes, the girls would convince me to join a round of hopscotch, and for a brief moment, I felt part of something.

The playground itself remains vivid in my mind. We called it the blacktop. It was just asphalt, hard and unforgiving, with two storm drains at either end and three jungle bars of different shapes towering over the pavement. There were no wood chips or rubber padding—just bruises and scraped knees.

Along the side were concrete ramps leading down to the basement, where old railroad car wheels sat rusting, their purpose a mystery.

I would wander from one spot to another, my eyes scanning the scene like a panning camera. In hindsight, I think that's why photography became so important to me—the camera was my pen, my way to capture the world when words failed me. But I didn't think of it that way.

I just observed. The girls skipping rope, the boys on the baseball field, bicycles lined up in neat rows by the chain-link fence. I watched it all without participating, existing on the edge of it.

By fourth grade, something shifted. Suddenly, the girls started chasing me around the playground. It was winter, and I wore a long stocking hat with a tassel—all the rage in those days. They loved trying to grab it.

The girls chasing me, their hands outstretched. I darted between them, weaving through the jungle bars, my heart pounding with exhilaration. For once, I was part of the game, the center of their attention. I wasn't being judged for my reading or writing; I was simply a kid having fun. Being chased felt different than competing—it was playful, and it meant I belonged.

Maybe that was why the moment stuck with me. That feeling of being part of something—of being seen, of mattering—was rare. And maybe, in some way, I spent the rest of my life chasing it.

Years later, when I landed in L.A., I felt it again—that sense of stepping into a world where I was part of the energy, where things just clicked. Leaving wasn't just leaving a city. It was leaving a place where, for a while, I felt like I belonged.

Winter in Cleveland brought its fair share of snow. Most kids came by bus or trudged on foot, but not me. I rode my bike. Snow didn't stop me; it made the ride more thrilling. I'd slam my coaster brake and send the back tire skidding out, carving patterns in the untouched white. Or I'd push through the drifts, the front tire cutting a single, satisfying track through the snow. I loved riding because it was something I could do alone, without needing a team, without rules or judgment. It was independence. It was freedom.

I would lock my bike at the rack and pause, breathing in the cold air, the playground a sea of white except for my solitary trail. It felt like a secret only I knew. No one else seemed to understand the magic in that quiet, private moment. Maybe being the only one to see it made it special. Maybe that feeling of solitude—of choosing my own path— was what truly made me happy.

Life Blew Apart

As I entered junior high, life took an unexpected turn, unraveling in ways I couldn't have foreseen. In just two short years, everything seemed to blow apart. It was the beginning of 1970. The 60s were over, and the world itself seemed to be shifting around me. The Beatles had broken up, and my parents' marriage was following the same path.

For most teens, change is expected, even welcomed. But for me, it was as if the ground had moved beneath my feet. Camp, once a refuge, ended as I grew too old to be a camper. Even my last summer there hinted at the divisions ahead, when tension boiled over between the free-spirited grooms and the by-the-book counselors at one of our final dances—a clash of long-haired rebels and clean-cut rule followers that felt like a symbol of the world outside, where old ways collided with new.

Woodstock had happened the year before, and protests against the Vietnam War were intensifying. It felt like change was happening everywhere but inside me. I watched my friends lean into the latest trends—bell bottoms, carefree laughter, and effortless conversations with girls—while I felt like a spectator, observing but never joining.

Their easy transformations felt foreign to me. While my friends transformed into cool kids with bell bottoms, and the girls—once so familiar—became distant and alluring, I felt out of step. I imagined some were dating, even having sex. But that wasn't my scene. And while the world was bursting with new ideas, I was left wondering where I fit into it all.

I found my place, though, in the junior high audio-visual department. Mrs. Morris had mentioned to the school how I'd helped with the video camera back in elementary school, and that got me into AV. It gave me an escape, something I was good at. Joining AV meant I didn't have to be stuck in homeroom with the others, trying to fit in.

Maybe I missed out on making new friends there, but being in AV felt like having a backstage pass to the school. We could roam the hallways without a hall pass, which I know others envied.

Our job was to deliver movie projectors to classrooms, set up the video camera to record events, and occasionally "preview" movies. We even had our own small office where we could hide away, a little haven away from the pressure of fitting in with everyone else. It got me out of study hall, too, and if the day was dragging, we could always turn on the TV and escape for a while.

One day, there was a knock at the door. It was Alan, an old friend from elementary school. He grew his hair long, past his shoulders, and there were rumors about him using drugs—but he was still Alan.

"Hey Jim, mind if I hang out and watch some TV?" he asked.

"Yeah, sure. Let's go next door," I said, leading him into the equipment room.

"Check this out," he said, muting the TV and playing music. "Isn't this cool to watch TV with music?" I left him gazing at the screen and headed to my next class. When MTV launched years later, I thought of Alan's quirky experiment.

My older brother, two years ahead of me, was also at junior high. For the first few weeks, I tried to meet up with him for lunch.

"Lunch today? I'll meet you by the third-floor stairs and we can head down. How's that?" he would say in the morning.

It seemed he liked making maneuvering down the crowded stairs a game as everyone in the school was heading to the cafeteria or their next class. He would dodge in and out through the crowd, running down the stairs like it was an obstacle course. He'd weave around the people, dodging left, jumping right, twisting his body in every direction to get ahead.

I kept up with him for a while, but I quickly lost sight of him. By the time I reached the cafeteria, thinking he would be waiting for me, he was nowhere to be seen. I did this a couple of times but ended up joining some of my Boulevard friends. It seems like he enjoyed losing me more than having lunch together.

That small lunch group, probably considered geeks, had been my companions for lunch before AV. I barely remember what we talked about, but I do recall our fascination with the school's computer—off-limits to all but the top math students. I never qualified. My grades were mediocre—I was easily distracted and rarely put effort into studying.

Despite the perks of being in AV, something still felt missing—especially social experiences like meeting girls. I rarely got invited to parties, so when one finally came along, I jumped at the chance. At John's birthday party, I wandered around the first floor alone until someone mentioned that everyone was downstairs.

In a dimly lit room, the muffled thump of music blended with hushed whispers. The air carried a warm, heavy scent—punch, sweat, and something unspoken. Couples huddled in corners, shadows moving in flickers from the dim light. The tension felt electric, and I stood frozen, a spectator to something I couldn't name.

My chest tightened with unease—like the disoriented feeling in Three Dog Night's *Mama Told Me Not to Come*. She hadn't, but in that moment, I understood the song's meaning: the raw confusion of stumbling into something bigger and wilder than expected.

Christmas Surprise

Mom always loved Christmas, and before seventh grade, it felt magical to me—the warmth of the tree lights flickering against frosted windows, the scent of cinnamon and pine filling every corner, and the cozy crackle of a fire while carols played softly from the record player.

By seventh grade, I began to see it differently. It wasn't just about joy anymore. It was also Mom's self-imposed pressure cooker of expectations and perfectionism that often tipped her over the edge.

That year, 1970, was particularly hard. Dad had moved out earlier that summer, and it was clear our family was in its final months of dissolving.

This Christmas would be the last one where Mom went all out with her decorating. Every ledge in the house was filled with creche scenes, little wooden carolers, snow-covered pine trees, each piece placed with her usual intricate touch.

The massive mirror over the fireplace became a painted winter wonderland, reflecting the Grandma Moses print hanging over the piano on the opposite wall. She spent hours on it, as if capturing that

49

perfect holiday scene could somehow revive a sense of peace our family had lost and perhaps, in some quiet way, the innocence of her own youth.

But beneath the surface, her obsession with making Christmas perfect came at a cost. By the time the holidays arrived, she was always mentally and emotionally drained. In the later years of their marriage, more than once, Christmas pushed her to the brink.

One year, she ended up in the psych ward, having driven herself to exhaustion, trying to make everything just right. I didn't fully understand it then, but I could sense that Christmas, which we kids loved, had become a weight too heavy for her to carry.

Christmas morning began as usual. While we were opening our presents, I noticed a cord running from under the loveseat.

"What is this cord?" I asked, curiously.

I followed it to the outlet, wondering where it led. Just as I started to lift the skirt of the couch, Mom saw me and said, "Oh, Jimmy, leave that alone, it's a surprise."

Not wanting to spoil anything, I backed off.

The tree, as always, was overflowing with gifts, creating a barrier of brightly wrapped presents that seemed almost impossible to get through. My siblings and I had our designated corners of the living room to stash our haul, and we tore through it all with the usual excitement. But even in the chaos of gift-giving, I could feel it, that tension simmering just beneath Mom's smile, the one I was beginning to recognize as a sign that something was off.

As we moved on to breakfast, the familiar spread of sticky cinnamon rolls with pecans, eggs, bacon, and hot chocolate, the kitchen was buzzing with excitement. We were chattering away about what we'd received, laughing, and reliving the morning's best moments.

Then, out of nowhere, Mom's mood shifted. She got up from the table and left the room. When she came back, she wasn't carrying the warmth of Christmas with her. Instead, she carried a tape recorder.

She slammed it onto the counter, her face stern and distant. "You spoiled kids! Just listen to yourselves," she snapped, pressing play.

The sounds of us opening presents, our laughter, the rustling of paper, filled the room, but now it felt chaotic and loud, stripped of all the joy we had felt just minutes earlier.

We all froze. No one said a word. I glanced at my siblings, but they were just as stunned as I was. The recorder kept playing, each sound that once symbolized Christmas cheer now seemed tainted by Mom's frustration. The air felt heavy, like all the excitement of the morning had been drained away in a matter of seconds.

A part of me, even then, felt sorry for her. I could see through her anger to the pressure she put on herself to make everything perfect. It was clear she had overdone Christmas again, and this year, instead of collapsing from the stress, she turned it on us.

At that moment, I didn't fully grasp the weight of her struggles, but I knew enough to feel something stir inside me, a mix of pity and the kind of love a child has for a parent, the kind that sees beyond the outbursts.

After a few moments, I quietly stood up and turned off the tape recorder. The room stayed silent. My siblings didn't move. Mom had already left the room, leaving us to sit with the aftermath of her outburst. The fun, the joy, it had all been sucked away.

As we sat there, finishing breakfast in silence, I couldn't help but feel a sadness settle in. Christmas, once so magical, had become something else entirely, something that took more from Mom than it gave her. It wasn't until years later that I fully understood the toll her mental health had taken on her, the breakdowns, and how they slowly tore apart the family I had known.

Olin School

I gasped for air as the plane broke through the thick clouds. The sun shone brilliantly in a sea of blue sky as the last hour of the day quietly passed. It had been gloomy all weekend, not the soft, drifting clouds but the heavy, dark winter kind that made everything feel oppressive.

I had spent the entire weekend cooped up in the silent house, sifting through old memories that seemed to cling to every object. The weight of it all pressed on my mind, and the isolation of not being able to communicate with anyone beyond the attorney left me feeling trapped in the past. It was a long, exhausting weekend. I'd barely made a dent, and in two weeks, I'd have to return to continue preparing the house for sale before spring.

I had brought my childhood folder with me on the flight back. I opened it, shuffling through its contents, and pulled out some old report letters from Olin School. They didn't use the standard report cards like public schools. Instead, each subject's teacher, referred to as the "Master", wrote personal evaluations, noting whether the student was putting in effort or slacking off. The Head Master also wrote individual letters, primarily to report on each student's progress in language skills, which was the school's primary focus since most of us were dyslexic and far behind in reading compared to other kids our age.

Reading through them, I was struck by the school's perception of me, especially in terms of how I interacted with my classmates. The Head Master noted, "Jim has been pleasant, courteous, and cooperative... he does not seem particularly close with his fellow students." Another letter read, "While he is not unfriendly, he has not... established close relationships with peers."

This has always been one of my biggest mysteries in life—why don't I have many close friends? Or maybe the real question is, why do most people act the way they do? I could never quite get into what the other guys were doing in their free time.

Some of them, the ones who might be called the jocks, would pretend they were soccer stars, kicking goals on the field. In study hall, they'd turn tables into football fields, folding a sheet of paper into a triangle and flicking it between goalposts made from outstretched thumbs and forefingers. I watched, but I never understood—what was the point? What did they get out of pretending? Was it practice? A social ritual? Just a way to pass time?

I suppose I had my own kind of pretending—framing the world through a camera lens, composing images in my mind long before I ever held a camera. But to me, that wasn't pretend. It was real. I wasn't acting like a photographer; I was seeing the world as one, even if few could appreciate the pictures I wanted to take.

In retrospect, maybe that was part of it. I was always watching— whether in real life or on a screen. As a kid, I spent hours in front of the TV, absorbing the way people talked, moved, reacted. Television didn't require participation; it only asked you to observe. And in a way, that's what I did best.

On weekends, while groups of boys disappeared into the woods, their voices fading into the trees, I took a different path. The valley stretched wide before me, silent except for the crunch of my boots over fallen leaves and twigs—some fresh and brittle, others softened by time. I ran my hand along the rough bark of a maple tree, tracing its ridges like a language I couldn't quite read. The wind moved the branches above, whispering secrets I wasn't meant to hear. But more often, I found myself bored, lying on my bed, sleeping away the hours, wishing for something to do.

I didn't expect to find answers to these questions as I flipped through the folder, but reading those letters brought back memories. Despite feeling trapped and isolated at a school that seemed stuck in the 1940s, I now look back on Olin with a sense of guarded fondness I wouldn't have imagined possible.

As the plane headed west, I watched the sun slip beneath the horizon, pulling the night sky behind it. The weekend caught up with me. My mind, cluttered with old memories and unanswered questions, finally gave in to the dull hum of exhaustion. I began to relax, thinking about my time at Olin. Soon, though, my thoughts faded, blending into the white noise of the plane as it soared through the twilight.

* * *

The drive to the small township in upstate New York to the family-owned and operated Olin School was a journey into a quieter, more peaceful place, far from the noise and confusion of home. As we approached the small township, I felt a sense of calm wash over me. The campus, tucked away in a lovely wooded valley, reminded me of the serenity I had once known at Red Raider Camp. It was a place of simplicity, with small country houses turned into classrooms and just a couple of brick buildings. Olin was different, and that difference gave me hope.

Arriving early on that September day, I found myself at Grant dorm, a brick fortress built to withstand the trials of teenage boys. The indestructible cinderblock walls, metal doors, and battleship linoleum floors spoke of durability and resilience. My room was small, but the view of the woods outside my window brought me comfort, a glimpse of tranquility that felt worlds away from the chaos I had left behind.

At home, my family life was fractured: constant battles between my siblings, the lingering tension of my parents' divorce, and the relentless noise of a divided house. Most of all, a public school system that failed to recognized the intelligence I had.

The wooded valleys surrounding Olin beckoned, offering the same peacefulness I had only known at camp. The woods promised a quiet refuge, an escape from the turmoil that had defined my everyday life.

When my mom left to drive home, I didn't feel sadness, just a sense of ambivalence, as if her departure marked the beginning of something necessary. Olin offered what public high school never could, a real chance to overcome my struggles with reading and spelling. For that, I was glad to be there. As I stood in the quiet aftermath of her leaving, the valley called to my soul, offering a sense of belonging that had long eluded me.

Later, when my roommate Dave arrived, the reality of this new chapter began to settle in. A light rain fell as we walked back from the dining hall, still finding our footing in this unfamiliar place.

As Dave unpacked and we got acquainted, our door suddenly flew open. Four seniors barged in, each more striking than the last.

"Hey, you guys new this year?" asked the guy in a yellow rain slicker, looking like a sailor straight out of Gloucester's Fisherman's Memorial. His rain hat, with its broad back brim, shielded his neck from the rain.

"I'm John," he said, grinning. "This is Mike and Brian. We live in Overlook House."

Overlook was the five-person dorm up by the ski hill, an aptly named house with a sweeping view of the valley. Mike had wild, curly hair and half-closed, sunken eyes that gave him a mysterious, almost aloof look. Brian, rugged and self-assured, wore a barn coat with his jeans tucked into chin-high L.L. Bean Maine hunting boots. They seemed like characters pulled straight from a TV show—larger than life, embodying an effortless coolness that captivated me.

"We came down to see our friend Peter. He lives down the hall," Mike added casually.

"What a rainy night," Brian said, shaking his head, droplets of water flying off as he did. "Ninth-graders?"

"Yep," Dave replied, glancing at me for reassurance.

They joked, laughed, and filled the room with an easy confidence that made them seem invincible—unfazed by the new school year that lay ahead.

As a ninth-grader, I looked at them with a mix of awe and aspiration. I could only hope that when I became a senior, I would be as cool and sure of my place in the world as they were in that moment.

Olin's campus was a unique blend of history and practicality, with its layout stretching along Graham Road and the winding waters of Pine Creek. At its core stood the Founders' Building, originally a barn that had transformed over the years with various wings and additions. I remember crawling into the attic once and discovering remnants of a pulley system, likely used to haul hay up into the loft—a faint echo of the building's rustic origins.

By the mid-1970s, the Founders' Building had become the heart of campus life, housing two study halls, the headmaster's office, business offices, and several small classrooms on the first floor.

Upstairs, dorm rooms were strictly off-limits to all but residents and their guests, with two doubles at each end of the hall, two singles in the center, and a shared bathroom equipped only with toilets and sinks—showers were reserved for the locker room in the basement and were usually only taken after sports practices, almost never at other times.

The basement, perpetually cold and damp, had its own utilitarian charm. In one corner sat the senior lounge, a space claimed by the oldest students, with the barber's room tucked right next to it, complete with a 1940s barber chair.

Down a narrow hallway was the shower room—a cramped, 10-by-10-foot space where six showerheads lined two adjacent walls. At any given time, eight to ten students squeezed in, jockeying for space. The room's stark, enclosed feel unsettled some. I remember a Jewish student once remarking that it reminded him of something from history he'd rather not think about. I chuckled at the bluntness of the comparison, but in hindsight, the comment lingered. There was something about Founders' basement—it felt cut off from the rest of the school, almost like a world of its own.

That sense of separation extended beyond the basement itself. Olin itself existed apart from the norms of other private schools. It lacked the polish and elitism often associated with such institutions, replacing them with a different kind of rigor.

For me, Olin was both a refuge and an isolating experience—a place where I belonged in ways I never had before, yet still felt apart from my peers. Across the hall from the showers, old wooden sports lockers stood in various states of disrepair, their doors hanging off their hinges, bearing the weight of years gone by.

Tucked beneath the creaky pine stairs that lead to the main study hall was the small school bookstore, stocked with supplies and essentials for students.

The Founders' Building's patchwork design, shaped by its barn beginnings and the haphazard additions adapted over the years, perfectly captured the essence of Olin. It was a place where history met the everyday realities of school life, where creaky floors and makeshift rooms mirrored the students' own journey of piecing together strengths and finding stability amid personal challenges. Despite its imperfections—or maybe because of them—the building resonated with a raw authenticity, a testament to the school's character and the perseverance it sought to instill in us.

The second study hall, tucked away in a wing of the Founders' Building, doubled as the school's makeshift library, with short bookshelves—just four feet wide and five feet tall—lining the walls between windows, though it barely resembled a library at all. It was nothing like the Boulevard library, where books stood proudly in neat rows, waiting to be explored.

Here, the collection was sparse, with most books dating back to the 1950s or earlier—torn, worn, and neglected—mirroring the struggles of students for whom reading was a battle. At the center of this so-called library sat a battered set of World Book Encyclopedias from 1950, with a couple of missing volumes—a relic of a bygone era and a testament to the school's focus on overcoming dyslexia, not fostering a love for reading.

For us, words were often adversaries, not gateways to adventure, and this library wasn't even worth a laugh. The tattered books, like the students, bore the scars of reading struggles. Pages were torn, spines broken—just like us, trying to read words we couldn't even spell. The worn and incomplete books reflected the gaps in our skills, making it nearly impossible to fully engage, much like our attempts to wrestle meaning from words that refused to make sense.

Can you imagine trying to learn in a library where even the books seemed to have given up?

Entering the Founders' Building through the front door was a privilege reserved only for Masters and seniors. Anyone else caught using it could face harsh consequences, a punch, or something even worse. Most students, therefore, entered through the basement, making their way up the ancient, well-worn cupped pine steps. These steps, marked deeply by time and frequent use, felt as though they might give way at any moment.

The narrow steep stairway, dimly lit by a faint glow from the windows in the door at the top and a bit of light rising from the basement below, created a shadowy passage. Along its sides, handrails made from old plumbing pipes provided a sense of stability. It was common to see students gripping these rails as they headed down the stairs, kicking their feet up with a mix of caution and playfulness—legs almost parallel to the stairs. This wasn't just about navigating the stairs but also a subtle dance of asserting one's place in the unspoken hierarchy of school life, all within the confines of this creaky old stairwell.

The first day of classes at Olin was an exhilarating experience. The school's country houses, now transformed into classrooms, featured weathered wooden floors and walls of knotty pine, exuding rustic charm. It was uncommon to have consecutive classes in the same building, turning each class change into an opportunity to step outside and breathe in the fresh valley air.

Throughout those first few weeks, and indeed during my four years, each moment spent outdoors felt like stepping through a living painting, where breathtaking views filled my heart with overwhelming gratitude. Not even rain or snow could dampen my spirits; armed with umbrellas and galoshes, I embraced the elements, finding joy in the rugged beauty that each season painted across the campus.

In my first year, I shared several classes with my roommate, Dave, and we quickly became friends. There was also Tom, a kid from my home town, who was in most of my classes. Tom and I often took the Greyhound bus home together during breaks, forging a connection through our shared background.

One of the most significant classes at Olin was Reading class. The Reading class was mandatory, with every student attending the class five times a week. I felt fortunate to have my Reading class taught by Bill Olin, the founder's son. Tom, Dave, and I were in the same Reading class, and we also sat together during night study halls.

Mr. Olin's classroom was distinctively set up with narrow but tall windows that filled two walls, opening up to views of tall maple trees that provided a cool shade from the hot sun. The classroom, like all the others had a blackboard, which was just that, four by eight-foot wooden panels painted flat black. Only the Headmaster's office / classroom had a real slate blackboard.

Mr. Olin sat in the corner of the two window walls, near a small bookshelf where he kept class books and the Readers' Digest for in-class reading. He favored a low swivel metal office chair that he liked to tilt back as far as possible.

The windows in the room were held open by clamps, and sometimes, if a window was accidentally knocked or the wall was bumped, the clamps would lose their hold, causing the window sash to slam shut, a surefire way to wake up anyone dozing off in the adjacent study hall.

Our group, including Dave, Tom, and two others, gathered around the map table in Mr. Olin's classroom. The table with its 4-foot diameter glass top under which a hand-painted world map was displayed. The glass had been cracked long ago, with years of dirt wedged into the crack, a testament to the table's age and the many students who had used it.

Mr. Olin greeted us with a no-nonsense, "Good morning, boys. Did you have any trouble finding your classrooms?"

He seemed more personable than most teachers I had known in public school, with his light blue and white striped seersucker sport coat, khaki pants, and preppy red and blue striped tie. His white hair gave him a distinguished look, though he didn't seem that old. His speech had a New England-ish lilt, which felt slightly foreign to my ears accustomed to Cleveland accents.

After the initial greetings, he began to explain the importance of Reading class, setting the tone for what would become a pivotal part of our education at Olin.

"Boys, the main reason you're here is to help you build your reading and spelling skills. As you do, your reading comprehension will improve as well. In this class, we're going to re-teach you how to read and spell."

Mr. Olin handed out a sheet of paper filled with letters and letter groupings. I recognized some of the vowels and combinations like 'gh,' 'ch,' 'oo,' and 'ou,' but there were also groupings like 'aste,' 'ould,' and 'eau.' Many of them had little numbers above, like in math when you square or cube a number.

"Boys," Mr. Olin continued, "this is a list of the most common letter combinations that make up the majority of words in the English language. Over your years here, you'll master all the combinations."

He explained something about diphthongs, where two vowels form one sound, and triphthongs, where three vowels make one sound. The first day of class was easy enough; we got to know each other and learned what lay ahead. I was eager to dive deeper into these sounds and letters. The list of sounds seemed vast, but they also held the key to becoming the better reader and speller I knew I could be. As the class ended, we headed out for our 10:00 break.

The next day in Reading class, Mr. Olin handed us some small cards—unlined 3x5 index cards, cut in half.

"Today, boys, we'll make your sound cards," he said.

I wondered why they weren't pre-made, like the math flashcards I used in fifth grade.

"You're probably wondering why we have you make your own cards," Mr. Olin said, noticing our curiosity. We all nodded.

"We've found that if you make them yourself, it helps you learn. You'll also value them more since you made them."

In those days, I didn't realize it, but this was an early example of multisensory learning—the idea that engaging multiple senses, like sight, touch, and movement, can help reinforce memory and understanding. By making the cards ourselves, we were absorbing the lesson in more ways than one.

"I'm going to give you your first five cards, and we'll practice and learn them before adding more," he continued.

This approach made sense to me.

"Tom, do you know what sounds 'a' makes?" Mr. Olin asked.

It seemed like a simple question, but I could see the others were just as uncertain as I was.

Tom replied, "'A' says /ă/ as in 'apple' and /ā/ as in 'hate.'"

Mr. Olin nodded and then helped us understand the sheet and what the small numbers meant.

"Actually, the letter 'a' has five sounds. Boys, do you see the little '5' at the top right of 'a' on the list? That indicates it has five distinct sounds. For each letter or group of letters, those numbers show how many sounds they can make. When two letters make one sound, we call them diphthongs, and when three letters make one sound, we call them triphthongs."

This information was enlightening—some of the mystery of spelling was finally being revealed.

I asked, "Sir, how do you know which sound to use?"

"Practice and learning these combinations," he replied. "That's as straightforward as we can make it. You'll get to know these combinations by heart, and you'll understand when to use each sound. And if you don't know a word or which sound to use, you can run through each sound until the correct one forms a recognizable word that fits the sentence."

"'A' has five sounds. To help you remember them, we use guidewords. Let's make your first reading card. On one side, write the letter 'a' and put a small '5' in the top right corner. On the back, write these words: 'Al hates a small spa.'"

I turned to Dave and asked, "How do you spell 'spa'?"

I was lost already.

Mr. Olin wrote the words on the board and explained each sound and its notation. The sounds could be 'long' or 'short,' but there were also 'faded' (indicated by double dots), 'tented' (marked with a ^ symbol), and more. He pronounced the guidewords and then the sounds the letters made.

"Al hates a small spa. Short 'a,' long 'a,' faded 'a,' tented 'a,' double-dotted 'a.' The faded 'a' sounds like a short 'u.' Tented 'a' sounds like 'aw' as in 'saw,' and double-dotted 'a' sounds like a short 'o.'"

It was a bit overwhelming, but I listened closely and repeated after him. After we each went around the table, practicing our first reading card—most of us getting the sounds somewhat correct—Mr. Olin introduced the next card.

"The second card for today will be 'e.' Write 'e' on the front of a new card and put a '3' in the top right corner. 'E' has three sounds. On the back, write 'Ed Stevens.'"

Again, I glanced at the others to see how to spell "Stevens." I thought, *How can I learn these cards when I can't even make them correctly?* It would have been so much easier if they were already made.

In Mr. Olin's reading class, the challenge was immediately apparent as he posed a question to the class.

"Who wants to say the sounds 'e' makes?"

Mike, bold and quick to respond, attempted the task but faltered on the third sound, defaulting to a short 'e' instead of the nuanced tone it required.

Mr. Olin intervened with patience and a clear teaching instinct. "Say 'Stevens' slowly. Listen to the last syllable," he instructed, pointing out the subtle but distinct sound of a faded 'e.'

He carefully pronounced each variant: "Ed Stevens—short 'e,' long 'e,' faded 'e.'"

He explored this idea further by pointing out how Americans often shorten or soften their pronunciation of certain words, using 'process' as an example.

"In the US, we tend to say 'pra-cess,' letting the vowel sound fade away. But in the UK or Canada, they pronounce it as 'pro-cess,' keeping the long 'o' clear and distinct."

This contrast emphasized the nuances of English pronunciation, making the lesson both informative and engaging.

As we practiced these sounds around the table, the task became increasingly manageable. Mr. Olin introduced us to the concept of diphthongs using 'boat' as a guideword to illustrate the long 'o' sound that "oa" makes. The session progressed to 'ck', with 'lock' as the guideword. Tom, initially puzzled as if expecting a catch, cautiously articulated the sound. "ck, lock, k," he said correctly, earning Mr. Olin's nod of approval.

The class went on like this, with Mr. Olin guiding us through the sounds, starting with 'a', then 'e', and so on. Each of us took turns pronouncing the sounds. Repeating them helped us get better at recognizing the phonemes, and it showed me that I wasn't the only one having a hard time. Seeing others struggle like I did, made me feel less anxious and more connected to them. As we worked together on these tricky sounds, we not only learned more effectively but also built a surprising sense of unity. It was comforting to realize that none of us were alone in our reading challenges.

On our third day in Reading class, we continued practicing with the cards we had made the previous day. As we each recited the letter, its guideword, and the corresponding sounds, Mr. Olin, leaning back in his swivel chair, corrected us with precision whenever we missed a sound.

His classroom was a haven of curiosity for me—especially the old map table, its thick lathe-turned legs sturdy under the weight of time. '54' was etched next to the creator's name, a small mystery that made me wonder who had sat here before me. The pine foot support bars were rounded and smooth from years of restless feet pressing against them, just as mine did now, shifting as I struggled through another reading exercise.

"The next card is for the letter 'i', which has three sounds," Mr. Olin announced.

I glanced around and noticed some classmates had written an uppercase 'i' while others used a lowercase 'i,' both marking a small '3' in the upper right corner to indicate its three distinct sounds.

Noticing the inconsistency, Mr. Olin said, "Make sure to use a lowercase 'i' and add the small '3' in the upper right corner to show its three sounds."

I quickly corrected my card.

"Jim, since your name is one of the guidewords, why don't you tell us the three sounds of 'i'?" he suggested.

My heart raced as I began, "'i,' Jim likes machines. (short i), (long i)..." My voice faltered, the pressure mounting as everyone watched me. The room's heat seemed to intensify, my palms slick with sweat. As I hesitated, my cheeks burning, I scanned the words, realizing the 'ine' in 'machines' hinted at a long 'i' due to the tunneling 'e.'

"Say 'machine' slowly," Mr. Olin guided, his voice steady and reassuring.

I stuttered at first, then pronounced, "(long e)," hesitantly.

"Yes," he confirmed with a nod. "Now, repeat the whole phrase."

Taking a deep breath, I managed, "'i,' Jim likes machines, (short i), (long i), (long e)."

"Excellent," Mr. Olin applauded. "It has three sounds: (short i), (long i), (long e). Remember, 'y' shares these same sounds."

"'Y'? But isn't 'y' a consonant?" Tom interjected, puzzled.

Mr. Olin smiled, seizing the teachable moment.

"Vowels are a, e, i, o, u, and sometimes y and w," he recited, his voice echoing slightly in the classroom.

Most of us paused at 'y,' but it was the mention of 'w' that caused a collective murmur of surprise.

"'W,' as in 'saw,' doesn't act as a simple consonant but as part of a diphthong, producing an 'aw' sound, which is a tented 'a,'" he explained, demystifying another layer of English's complexities

This revelation about 'w' and 'y' was intriguing, and as Mr. Olin continued, I found myself appreciating the structure he brought to the seemingly chaotic English language. Although we had made only a few cards, their value was becoming clear. Inspired by this newfound understanding, I decided to perfect my Reading cards during the next study hall, aiming for neatness and precision in both layout and handwriting, an act of taking control over my dyslexic challenges, one beautifully crafted card at a time.

In addition to the basics of reading, we were also taught spelling and vocabulary. While it might seem like these are naturally linked, for a dyslexic, they require a different approach to master. Mr. Olin introduced us to spelling using what he called "spellables"—essentially breaking words down into syllables. For example, the word "separate" becomes "sep-a-rate." This method allowed us to focus on smaller chunks instead of the entire word. When we say "separate," the "a"s often blend and sound like a short "e," but by breaking it down—"sep" (short 'e'), "a" (long 'a'), "rate" (long 'a')—it becomes much easier to spell.

Another example is "Wednesday." It's easy to overlook the first "d" when saying it, but breaking it down to "Wed-nes-day" reveals the spelling in a more straightforward way. This technique of exaggerating each syllable gave us a practical tool to tackle even the trickiest words.

We also dedicated a lot of time to expanding our vocabulary—not just to improve our spelling, but to grasp the parts and origins of words. We learned about prefixes and suffixes, such as how the suffix "ous" means "full of," as in "famous" (full of fame) or "adventurous" (full of adventure).

Mr. Olin would emphasize that knowing these patterns made it easier to decode unfamiliar words. He also explained how some prefixes change depending on the root word to make pronunciation smoother.

For example, the prefix "in," meaning "in, on, or not," transforms into "ir" in words like "irregular" because "inregular" would be awkward to pronounce. We explored word roots, tracing them back to Latin origins and learning how these influences shaped English spelling.

By breaking words down into their components, we could see how different languages and dialects contributed to their evolution. Understanding these building blocks gave us a toolkit for decoding language, making unfamiliar words feel a little less daunting. This was phonics on steroids, the method of understanding how letters and sounds come together to form words.

Over the next four years, I immersed myself in the inner workings of the English language. It took that long for me to finally feel some confidence in my reading and spelling abilities. Even then, my processing speed remained slow— reading was never easy. My writing gradually improved, especially when I gained access to a typewriter— where I only had to press the letters instead of painstakingly forming them by hand—and later, a PC, where I could rearrange the sentences for a more cohesive flow. Once, a very studious person even complimented me, saying I could spell unfamiliar words better than she could.

Reflecting on my time at Olin, I realize that it wasn't just language skills I gained—it was also a sense of structure and routine that shaped my life. The school's strict daily schedule, from wake-up calls to study periods, established a rhythm that brought stability and comfort. In hindsight, I didn't recognize it, but the discipline of that routine was exactly what I needed. The predictable flow of the day helped me manage the anxiety that often accompanied learning challenges.

Now, decades later, I unconsciously maintain a similar structure. I need my daily schedule—when I wake up, eat, work, exercise, and so on—to be consistent throughout the week. It's not that every day must be identical, but I feel at ease when tasks like grocery shopping or doing laundry happen at the same time each week.

It's as if the discipline of routine frees up mental energy that would otherwise be spent on decision-making. Maybe it's because these structured patterns take away the need to think about small details. In that discipline, I find freedom. That's a lesson I unknowingly carried from Olin: a routine isn't confining; it's a steady, dependable anchor.

Mischief

While I was at Olin to tackle my struggles with reading and spelling, life at school had its moments of fun and mischief—ones I observed or quietly joined, but never led.

Every afternoon, all students were required to participate in a sport—there was no opting out. The school was too small to field teams otherwise, so everyone played. With no athletic building or indoor facilities, afternoon activities took place outside, rain, snow, or shine. That was no problem for me. In fact, I welcomed it. My time at camp and my morning paper route had conditioned me to all kinds of weather, and I believed it built strength in more ways than one.

Fall meant soccer, spring brought lacrosse, and winter offered a mix of outdoor activities. The school had even cleared land on a hill in the valley for a ski slope, though snow was never guaranteed. When it did snow, the first task wasn't skiing—it was sidestepping up the hill to pack the snow down. By the time the slope was ready, there was often little time left before late afternoon classes to actually ski.

One snowy winter night, after lights-out, I heard a tapping on my window. I opened the curtain to see Dale. At the time, I was living in Founders', which shared a flat roof with his room. He had climbed across to invite me on a midnight toboggan ride down the school's ski hill.

"What's up?" I whispered.

"Hey, let's go tobogganing," he whispered back, grinning. "The Masters are done for the night. We've got at least an hour before they check on us."

"Heck yeah!"

"Climb over to my window, and we'll head out through the Headmaster's office."

Dale's dorm room was above the office and part of that addition. Like I said, Founders' Building was additions upon additions.

We quietly closed the door behind us and snuck across campus, grabbed the toboggan from Overlook's garage, and trudged to the top of the powdery hill. As we sped down, the freshly fallen snow flew up in bursts, covering the front of the toboggan, spraying over our heads, and blinding us. We had to turn our heads to the side just to catch glimpses of our surroundings as the dark silhouettes of trees at the bottom loomed closer.

Somehow, we managed to stop just in time, collapsing into laughter and gasping for breath under the moonlit sky.

Study hall offered its own share of low-key humor. Occasionally, a student would nod off at their desk, worn out from the day's routines.

One time, Sam Weston sat against the wall, creating a perfect three-sided space. He was tilted back in his chair on two legs for maximum comfort. His books were carefully arranged in front of him, making it hard to tell if his eyes were open or not. It looked like he was studying, but many of us recognized the tactic—we knew he was catching some Zs.

That night, Mr. Kane, the upper school English Master—known for using his deep, booming voice when reading plays aloud in class—spotted Sam and walked over. He lowered his head to peer past Sam's book barricade to confirm his suspicion. Sure enough, he was asleep. But how deeply?

Mr. Kane quietly motioned for the rest of us to stay silent. With exaggerated care, he removed each book one by one and signaled those nearby to move away. We all caught on immediately and were more than happy to play along.

Then, with his booming voice turned up to nine, he bellowed, "Mr. WesTON! Would you like to join us in study hall?!"

Sam jolted awake, throwing himself off balance and crashing to the floor. He looked up, dazed and confused, still trying to process being so rudely awakened.

Another time, my roommate convinced me to join a weekend hike through the woods to a ravine. I hadn't expected much—a quiet walk, maybe a chance to clear my head—but when we arrived, I froze.

A group of students huddled around a campfire, beer in hand, laughing and shouting over the crackling flames. And there, skewered on sticks and held above the fire, was the unmistakable Sunday dinner roast beef. I stood there, stunned. I had heard rumors about these secret gatherings—the whispered stories of midnight escapades and rebellious pranks—but I had never been invited. Not since that late-night toboggan ride the year before had I been part of something so daring.

Still, this felt different. I didn't know what to say or do. The whole scene felt surreal, like I had stumbled into a hidden world just beyond the reach of the school's carefully controlled routine.

Some students dared each other to swing over the ravine on a rope tied to a high tree branch, their laughter echoing through the woods. I watched in silence, still trying to process it all. This wasn't just mischief; it was their version of freedom—a small, defiant taste of adventure in a place that demanded structure and discipline.

Oddly, I can recall every detail of that afternoon—the smell of the smoke, the chill in the air, the nervous thrill that came with knowing we shouldn't be there—but none of my own interactions. I was in shock, a quiet observer to something that felt both thrilling and forbidden.

Needless to say, the dining hall was noticeably short on roast beef that Sunday.

11th Grade Unrest

The mid-1970s were a period of upheaval—energy crises, the fallout from the Vietnam War, and the aftermath of President Nixon's resignation created a general atmosphere of uncertainty. Life at Olin was no different. During my third year, the tension on campus shifted from mild discontent to outright hostility. We all felt stifled. The school was in financial turmoil, and as a result, extracurricular activities had been cut, leaving little to break up the monotony.

If that wasn't bad enough, dating and any semblance of a typical high school social life were nonexistent. That summer, I joined a coed geological trip out west, which only made me more aware of what I was missing at this all-boys school. My desire to be anywhere but there grew stronger.

The choices for Saturday night at Olin were limited. While I imagined kids in public high school were out on dates or driving around with friends, our options were rigid. We could either stay on campus for study hall or go into town to watch a movie, wearing our required coat and tie—a rule that made us stand out even more.

Stepping off the bus on Main Street in front of the theater, we weren't just boys going to a movie; we were Olin students—marked by our attire separating us from everyone else. Maybe it was the school's way of keeping tabs on us, or maybe it was about maintaining a certain image. Either way, before the film started, we had to check in with the on-duty Master, who made sure we attended the movie.

Most of my classmates took the usual path—movie night, a brief escape from campus. But I had a different Saturday night ritual. Unlike most students at Olin, I couldn't afford the laundry service, so every Saturday, while they sat in the dark watching a film, I was at the laundromat, waiting for my clothes to cycle through. While they swapped jokes and stories, I sat alone, listening to the rhythmic hum of the machines, the scent of warm detergent filling the air.

While waiting for the wash cycle to finish, I often wandered over to the doughnut shop and treated myself to a doughnut and hot chocolate. Deloris worked behind the counter, finishing the late batch of doughnuts and stacking coffee mugs in the washer under the counter. She was in her thirties, sharp but kind, her voice carrying over the low hum of the shop.

There was usually one steady customer—a guy who always seemed to be there on Saturday nights, nursing a coffee, chatting with her through the quiet shift. I was never really part of their conversations, more of a presence in the background, but I liked being there. It felt normal, like a scene from a movie about a diner.

Because of my coat and tie, my interactions in town were limited. People knew of Olin, but they didn't engage with us. We were from *that* school for boys who couldn't read—the ones sent away, separated from the rest of the world. No one asked about our lives or invited us into theirs.

Years later, I heard that some of my classmates had relationships with girls in town. It surprised me—not just because Olin felt so cut off from everything, but because the idea of dating was foreign to me. Maybe it was because the school was all boys, or maybe it was just me, but I left Olin with little understanding of girls or how relationships even worked. Dating seemed like something that belonged to public school.

Kids my age on the outside wore their hair long and followed the latest fashions. While I couldn't pull off most of those styles, the fact that we had our individuality stripped away only added to the resentment.

Haircuts were mandatory. Fred, the barber, made weekly visits to campus to ensure that every head was kept neatly trimmed—hair above the collar. On haircut days, we all helped each other remember whose turn it was. To squeeze out an extra half inch, we'd wear the lowest-collared shirts we could find and loosen our ties. It became a small act of rebellion, trying to keep our hair just a little longer than the rule allowed.

There weren't many activities or clubs that truly interested me. It wasn't a pleasant place to be, but photography caught my attention, so I tried joining the yearbook staff. Not having my own 35mm camera put me at a disadvantage, but that didn't end up mattering much—the staff seemed more interested in experimenting with growing plants in the darkroom than actually making a yearbook.

Even there, I didn't feel like I belonged. But as a dyslexic, I couldn't deny that being at Olin was helping me gain the tools I needed to read. That, at least, was something.

It was easy to get caught up in the negativity swirling around campus. I longed for some sense of autonomy, especially when twelfth graders were treated the same as seventh graders. I reached a breaking point one evening and called my mother.

"Hi, Mom."

"I'm doing well in my classes."

"But school isn't that good. There's nothing I like here. We're so confined. Little to no interaction outside this tiny valley. Everyone seems angry at the school. It's like a prison at times. There's no funding for field trips. I want to leave."

"I'd go back to public school."

"I've learned all the Reading class sounds. I feel better about reading and spelling. I just don't like it here."

She had worked so hard to get me into the school, sacrificing so much. When I told her how I felt, she suggested I talk things over with my father. The idea unsettled me. My parents had divorced, and Dad was living his own life. He seemed so distant, so removed from mine.

I hung up the phone and walked back to my dorm, her words — *go ask your father* — echoing in my mind like a cruel taunt. Lying in bed that night, the weight of those words pressed down on me. A bitter truth surfaced: I didn't know my father. The thought was overwhelming, and as it settled in, I cried quietly as I fell asleep.

That truth cut deep. I had wasted so many chances to connect with him, choosing the glow of the TV over his company. But it wasn't just the TV that kept me inside — it felt safer there.

Outside, every attempt seemed to end in failure. If Dad wanted to play ball, I couldn't catch or throw. When he worked on his car, I'd watch as he topped off the battery with water or checked the oil. Wanting a better view, I balanced on my bike beside his car, steadying myself with a hand on the hood—until I wobbled, lost my grip, and scraped the car's paint. It seemed that every time I ventured out, I let him down. Watching TV meant I couldn't fail, couldn't disappoint him—or myself.

Each time he tapped on the window, gesturing for me to come outside and join him, I stayed planted, staring at the screen unable to tear myself away. Realizing what I had let slip through my fingers felt like a punch to the gut. That night, it hit me hard: I wasn't just missing independence—I was missing a relationship with my father.

Commencement

At the start of 12th grade, I had tried returning to public school. The shift from Olin, with its 80 students and familiar structure, to a sprawling high school with over 800 kids had been overwhelming. It wasn't just the size—it was the expectations, the rigid requirements, and a system that didn't seem to know what to do with someone like me. Within weeks, I realized I wouldn't make it to graduation there. Humbling myself, I asked to go back to Olin.

Olin had become my safety net after the disaster of public school. The transition back wasn't easy. Olin was challenging, and its expectations pushed me in ways I didn't always appreciate. But at least I wasn't falling through the cracks. Here, I had a chance. I still wanted out—desperately—but I also knew I owed it to myself to finish strong.

Commencement finally arrived in May, but I hadn't met all the requirements to graduate. I failed American History—not by a narrow margin, but with a dismal 47 percent.

The Master handed out lists of names and dates as if they should mean something on their own. There was no context, no narrative, nothing to tie it all together, so I couldn't make sense of it. They were just empty facts that refused to stick.

Despite that failure, Dad and Gram came to see the ceremony—a rare treat to have them both there. Oddly, Mom wasn't present, even though she had been the one who found Olin for me.

I showed Dad and Gram around campus, pointing out the different buildings and talking about the sports I played. They watched as I participated in a school lacrosse game between the JV and varsity teams—a simple exhibition for the parents. The school had endured another losing season, but for once, losing didn't bother me. I was just glad to finally be done with Olin, ready to leave and move forward with life.

When the game ended, Dad pulled his car around to my dorm to help gather whatever I couldn't fit into my two suitcases. I would be taking the bus home in two weeks, after the New York Regents exam—the last thing standing between me and a diploma.

The graduation ceremony was simple and small, like Olin itself. Just two flags—the American and Canadian—fluttered above the gathering. Mr. Olin had added the Canadian flag years earlier to acknowledge the growing number of students from Canada, their tuition keeping the school alive.

The six of us that made up the senior class stood in front of the flags, along with a dozen or so guests. There was no grand music, no large crowds. And honestly, I liked it that way.

The two heads of the school gave short speeches, thanked everyone for coming, and made polite remarks about our futures. Diplomas would be mailed later, after we took our Regents exams.

It wasn't hard to catch the implied message in the Head Master's remarks—some of us, like myself, hadn't yet met all the requirements to graduate. There was no assumption that we were in the clear. My mind immediately went to the couple of post-graduate students who needed another year to complete the school's required courses.

Not me! *No way*, I thought.

That was it. A brief, unpretentious moment, and then Dad, Gram, and I were off to a restaurant in the nearby town. It had always been my favorite place to eat with Dad, and this time was no different. The prime rib and mashed potatoes with au jus sauce were as good as ever, and I especially enjoyed spending time with Gram.

The following day, Monday, it was back to reality. The start of the final two weeks. At 6:45 a.m., the master was already banging on the metal doors of Grant dorm, just like every morning for the past four years. There was no time to dwell on graduation. I had one mission: pass the Regents, stick it to the US History master whose teaching style made no sense to me, and finally get out of Olin for good. The Regents were my salvation, the key to escaping the worst year I had endured.

In New York State, the Regents exams determined whether you passed a subject or not. You could have gotten straight A's in the class, but if you failed the Regents, you failed the subject. In my case, the reverse was true: fail the class but pass the Regents, and you still passed the subject. That loophole was my saving grace, and I clung to it like a lifeline.

Regents' period was the best time to be at the school. It was early June, and the valley was alive with warm breezes and the fresh scent of cut grass that added a lightness to the days. After lunch, we usually played softball—true lazy summer games with plenty of laughter and no one taking things too seriously.

As a senior, I was ready to leave, eager to step into the world and try something new. During that first week, a few of the guys invited me to take a walk in the woods down by the river along the perimeter of the school.

They pulled out a joint, and though I'd avoided pot all my years at Olin, something about that day felt different. They assured me it would help me relax before the ball game. I was the pitcher—no one else wanted the job—and to my surprise, they were right. Whether it was the pot or simply the power of suggestion, I felt more at ease, freer to joke around and join in the nonsense of the moment.

The smoking rail was where students gathered between classes, after meals, and whenever there was time to spare. It was nothing more than three sections of a split-rail fence along the driveway to the dining hall, overlooking the Lower 40. Officially, it was the only place on campus where smoking was allowed, but more than that, it was a social hub—a place to unwind, trade stories, and watch the world go by.

But the most vivid memory from that period had nothing to do with cigarettes or pot.

June often brought late-day rain showers, and one evening, a group of us leaned against the smoking rail after dinner, waiting for study hall to start. The rain had passed during the meal, leaving behind the rich, clean scent of wet grass and warm pavement. The air was thick with humidity, carrying the earthy aroma of damp soil and the faint tang of rain evaporating off the cement walkways. Droplets still clung to the leaves, refracting the fading light like scattered bits of glass. Now, as the sun broke through the lingering clouds, the valley was bathed in a golden glow, the mist rising like breath from the ground.

We sat there, watching the sky shift, when suddenly, a rainbow began to form.

At first, it was faint, just a shimmer in the mist rising from the fields. Then, as we watched, the colors sharpened—deep reds, electric oranges, and a vivid indigo so rich it looked almost unreal. The arc stretched high, and the end of it seemed to land right in the middle of the athletic field, 50 yards away, the heart of campus.

For a moment, none of us spoke. We just stared, wide-eyed, before breaking into half-laughs and nudging each other. "You think there's actually a pot of gold out there?" someone joked. Another guy pretended to lunge forward as if he were about to run and find out.

None of us did, of course, but for a few seconds, we all believed in the possibility.

Years later, I came to understand that old saying in a different way. The gold was at the end of the rainbow; it was here all along. Olin had given me the tools I needed—the gold I'd been searching for—to sound out words and read.

Still, as relaxed as the days felt, I remained focused on one thing: finishing that Regents exam and leaving Olin behind. I took practice tests every day, morning and night, sometimes doing two full three-hour exams a day. The tests were mostly multiple choice, what we called "multiple guess," and I was confident I could pull it off.

The day of the exam finally came—June 9th. Five of us were driven to a local public school to take the test. I had arranged for a taxi to pick me up right after the exam, my bags already packed and waiting.

I walked in with the others but quickly lost track of where they went. The proctor checked off my name and handed me the exam booklet and answer sheet. I took my seat and waited for the go-ahead.

"You can start now. Please open your test booklet and begin," the proctor said.

I folded back the cover and skimmed the instructions—as if I needed to. They were the same instructions I had read over the past two and a half weeks.

I began working through the questions, reading them one by one and answering them one by one. I rarely went back to review my answers. I figured if I didn't know something by test day, I wasn't going to figure it out now.

Slowly, I worked my way through the exam. A couple of students finished early, turned in their tests, and walked out. I could only picture myself doing the same soon.

Finally, I reached the last question. The clock showed I still had time left. I thought briefly about reviewing my answers—but decided I was done. It was what it was.

By 11 o'clock, I handed in my exam with a surge of exhilaration. I knew I had passed. And just like that, I was done.

I left the exam room without looking back, climbed into the waiting taxi, and headed straight for the Greyhound bus station.

The Buffalo bus station was a place I would be glad never to see again. It was worse than an airport—crowded, loud, and filled with strange characters. The sharp smell of stale coffee and diesel fumes hung in the air, blending with the sour stench of unwashed clothes and spilled beer. The flickering fluorescent lights buzzed overhead, casting a harsh glow on the scuffed floors and plastic seats that had seen better days.

This was nothing like the quiet, secluded valley of Olin. Here, bag ladies shuffled by, pushing carts piled high with belongings wrapped in tattered plastic bags. A disheveled man with a wild beard and vacant eyes slumped in a corner, clutching a bottle wrapped in a paper bag. Every few minutes, the echo of an argument or a slurred outburst pierced through the constant hum of voices and footsteps.

Tom and I used to see one guy every time we were there. He wore a ratty old trench coat with pockets bulging with booze bottles, mumbling incoherent strings of thought to himself: *"Well, we ought to, but wait, wait, if we did, we-e-e-e... No, wait, he knows, but why..."*

Back then, seeing someone muttering to themselves felt unsettling. Today, you'd assume they had a phone in their ear, but in the mid-'70s, it was just plain weird.

Bus stations had a different kind of weirdness, and I was ready to leave that behind, too. I got my ticket with fifteen minutes to spare, saw to it that my bags were loaded, and boarded the bus. I tossed my carry-on bag onto the rack above the seats across from me so I could keep an eye on it without getting up, then settled in for the ride.

The exam had been just one more hurdle, something to complete before I could be free.

As the bus pulled out of Buffalo, I stared out the window, watching the chaotic rhythm of the city—the blur of taxis honking, people rushing by, and street vendors calling out to passersby—but my mind was already elsewhere. I took one last look at the city where I'd spent the past four years. The skyline had changed since I first arrived—new construction rising everywhere.

I knew every turn of the bus route by heart now. The same streets and buildings I had seen countless times before flickered past, familiar yet distant. As the bus merged onto the highway, leaving Buffalo behind, I leaned back and closed my eyes.

* * *

"Ladies and gentleman the captain has turned on the seatbelt sign, please return to your seat, put all electronics away, bring your seatback to the upright position and prepare for landing in Denver, Colorado."

James S. Harper

Finding My Way

Monday morning came quickly. I was grateful for the two-hour time difference, which allowed me to unpack and get a full night's sleep before the work week started. The trip to Cleveland and going through all of Mom's clutter had stirred up so much of the past. It was haunting to sit in silence all weekend, sifting through old memories.

As I unpacked boxes in the apartment I had just moved into after separating from my wife, I thought of the notebook I'd kept during my Steamboat adventure twenty-five years ago. I had felt so together back then, with insights that shaped the foundation of my life. I was twenty when I started writing in it, and I liked to think of it as my life's blueprint.

But reading my year-end Olin reports brought up something I had never fully understood about myself: Why was I always on the edge, looking in? It wasn't alarming—I had always thought I was just independent. I enjoyed being around people and doing things with them, but there was always something more going on beneath the surface. I couldn't quite understand why they behaved the way they did, and I chalked it up to the games people play.

That idea—that people moved through life playing games I didn't fully grasp—stayed with me, surfacing in unexpected ways as I navigated new environments. But clarity wasn't always easy to hold onto. I had once believed I could shape my own path, but life has a way of pulling you into places you never expected.

For years, I had avoided the corporate world, but after my dream career in photography faded, I had no choice. In my mid-30s, I entered corporate America for the first time, where my young looks helped me blend in. Most people assumed I was in my twenties, which gave me a strange advantage.

Starting in 1994, I worked as a PC technician for several large corporations. But I didn't see myself as a typical office worker. IT felt more like my old AV crew in junior high—essential but invisible, running things behind the scenes while the rest of the office played their roles in the corporate theater. I roamed between departments like Accounts Payable, HR, and Shipping, always moving but never settling. I was in the corporation but never of it.

That distance gave me an interesting perspective. I watched how the system worked, how people maneuvered for promotions, how meetings filled time but rarely accomplished anything. The logic of it all escaped me—why did everyone accept these rituals without question? But then again, I'd never been one to play along just because everyone else did.

At one point, I stepped into a supervisory role in an IT department. I thought it would be a step up, a natural progression in my career. Instead, it felt like stepping into quicksand. I took a hands-off approach, believing people should be self-motivated, but some of the younger techs constantly pushed back. "Why do I have to do this?" they'd ask, expecting rewards for tasks that should have been routine. Managing them felt like an endless negotiation, and the stress of trying to balance expectations with reality weighed heavily on me.

I'll never forget when the president of the company told me to make things rough for the unmotivated employees—to push them so hard they'd quit. It was easier to force them out than to fire them and deal with compensation. The corporate machine had little patience for inefficiency, and even less for people. Ironically, when my position was being phased out during a corporate takeover, they did the same to me. The pressure mounted, expectations became impossible, and the message was clear: resign, or be pushed out.

That experience left no doubt in my mind—corporations had no real loyalty to their employees. The ideals of job security, pensions, and lifelong careers, if they ever truly existed, were relics of a bygone era.

By now, it was common knowledge that employees were valued only as long as they served a purpose. Once profitability dictated otherwise, even the most dedicated workers were expendable. The corporate world was no longer about mutual loyalty but about navigating a system where individuals had to advocate for themselves.

At one point, I thought having a pension plan would be fantastic, a symbol of stability. But I learned that pensions were just another way to lock you into the company, to make sure you worked harder and longer hours. They were a kind of ransom.

Still, there was some freedom in this new world. No longer locked into one corporate culture, I realized I could grow and move to different companies, following my passion as it evolved. When I couldn't move up as a PC technician, I found a system administrator position at another corporation, finally shedding the old shell, like a crab that grows too large for its current home.

At twenty-one, I had written, "Know who you are before conforming to society's standards." Those words became a blueprint for my life, shaping my choices and values. I realized I didn't need to fully immerse myself in the establishment to find happiness.

While many thrive on rules and conformity, I discovered that what I truly needed was structure and order—a framework that made sense, not just rules for the sake of rules. My boyhood paper route had already taught me that running my own business wasn't my path. Instead, working in IT allowed me to engage with the corporate world without being consumed by it, maintaining my independence while embracing the structure I relied on.

I loved working in groups, but the corporate world felt different from my time in L.A., where creative people often collaborated without ego. The past four years had been like that—working at a small engineering site with just twenty people, all working toward a common goal. But then we were sold, and the acquiring company did what acquirers do— restructure and dismantle.

This additional stress was the last thing I needed. I was already navigating the emotional fallout of a divorce, traveling fifteen hundred miles to clean out and sell my mother's home, and managing the overwhelming responsibility of her care, which my siblings had abandoned me to handle alone. As if that weren't enough, they were now threatening me with lawsuits, adding to the weight of an already unbearable situation.

On top of all this, my work environment had turned increasingly hostile. Leaving Denver for the weekend offered a brief escape, but it stirred up far too many memories from days gone by, leaving me emotionally frayed and exhausted.

I started going through my boxes, tossing out items as I went. Cleaning out Mom's house must have inspired me to do some house cleaning of my own. It felt good, but I was also searching for that notebook. I finally found it, tucked away in a cardboard file box from the office supply store.

The box held all the writing I'd done in my early twenties. I remembered Miss Fox, one of my childhood tutors, telling me to keep a pad of paper by my bed to jot down my thoughts. As I flipped through the notebook, I realized how much of what I wrote felt like bold ideas for a twenty-year-old. Twenty-five years later, I couldn't help but wonder what had become of that person. I carried the notebook over to the couch, sat down, and began to look through it.

The notebook was a simple 9 ½ by 6-inch, 150-sheet, three-subject spiral notebook. The cover had several notes scribbled across it. By the manufacturer's printed label, "3 Subject Notebook," I had written, "Me, Myself & I." Next to "College Ruled," indicating the type of lined pages, were two sets of comments. One in blue ink: "No they don't," and a later one in black: "But a good place to learn." I think that was motivated by the first college I attended, which had denied me what they'd promised.

Now, I see that I was trying to make sense of the neurotypical world, constantly wondering where I fit in. At the time, I didn't have the language to explain it, but I was seeking patterns, categories—ways to understand the behaviors of others and how I might fit into their world.

It was all there, laid out in the spiral-bound notebook I had started writing in during my last semester of my first college. At the top center of the front cover, I had written, "Life is the Drug,". In the upper right corner was the phrase "Increase Your Awareness," and below that, "It's time to get serious about what you want & don't want—STYP, UYK." These acronyms were my way of organizing the chaos around me: STYP stood for "Stick To Your Plan," and UYK was "Use Your Knowledge."

I had a deep need to categorize people too, as if sorting them would help me understand the social world I couldn't fully access. On the upper part of the cover, I had written a section titled "Types of People":

Those who appear nice but aren't
Those who appear nice and are
Those who appear mean but aren't
Those who appear mean and are
Those who are nice but will be mean if treated mean

It was a reflection of how much I struggled with reading people's true intentions. Below that list, I had written:

There are those who act nice,
And there are those who are nice.
Which are you? Answer truthfully.

Even then, I was trying to map out human behavior in a way that would make sense to me. It was as though I could break the world down into pieces, analyze it, and maybe find a place where I could fit in.

I must have unconsciously known that my life was shifting. College wasn't the answer I had hoped it would be, and with no real guidance from my high school, and only minimal direction from my parents, I began constructing a world of my own. I was searching for perspectives that resonated with the changes I sensed within myself.

When I opened the notebook to the first divider page, paperclips lined the top, holding together fragments of my thoughts and reflections. The first thing I saw was a poem I had written—an early declaration of something new beginning:

Today I begin a new
Life of wonderment
Seen by a few
Adorned by many
For the peacefulness
That life's blueness

Soon turns happy
And things flow for you
With exuberance and amazement.
Today I begin anew.

On another page, I had written quotes from Robert Frost:

"How a poem is created: It begins in delight and ends in wisdom... it assumes direction with the first line laid down, it runs a course of lucky events, and ends in... a momentary stay against confusion."
"Go it your own way. You will be better for it."
"Do not turn from a dreamer into a schemer."
"See the way clear, and then go plowing ahead."

I was searching for direction, and though no one had laid it out for me, Frost's words seemed to point the way, offering me a kind of wisdom I hadn't received from the adults in my life. I was creating a map, one filled with other people's insights and my own reflections, trying to make sense of who I was and where I was headed.

As I flipped through the notebook, memories came flooding back. This was where I'd poured my thoughts while venturing out into the world, approaching my 21st birthday.

The entries weren't linear; some sections were dedicated to specific topics, while others started with an idea and left open spaces for later reflections. I remembered my quirky habit of flipping the notebook upside down to avoid resting my hand on the metal spiral. Sometimes I only wrote on the right-hand pages, then flipped the notebook to use the backs, keeping the spiral comfortably on the left. Writing with your hand pressing against those metal rings was uncomfortable, to say the least.

College: Take One

It was June 16th when I received a letter from the secretary at Olin. I had passed the history class, and to my surprise, I had missed making honors by only two points. Not bad for someone who had gotten 47 percent during the regular school year. I had made it out of high school. My graduation was confirmed, and I knew I would never return to Olin as a student. But now that I was done, the question loomed: What now?

I hadn't received much, if any, counseling about college while at Olin. All I knew was that college was the expected next step, but I needed a better reason than that to go back to school. I had just spent four years immersed in reading, writing, and arithmetic, and going back to school just because it was "what you did" wasn't enough.

I was eighteen. This was my life now. What did I want to do with it? What did I want to pursue? The only thing that interested me was photography—or more accurately, owning a 35mm SLR camera. Some of the guys at Olin had them, and I had been fascinated. All the dials and levers, the way you could change lenses and completely transform the view from wide angle to telephoto—it intrigued me.

But I needed a job, and quickly. I was living with Mom, and Dad had made it clear that I needed to pay my own way. He was right. But I had no clue where to find a job.

During my time at Olin, I had lost touch with everyone at home. The kids I grew up with had moved on, and I hadn't been close to any of them anyway. My struggles with reading and everything else left little room for strong friendships. On top of that, Mom had moved twice while I was at Olin, further disconnecting me from the kids I once knew. So when I came home, I found myself in a different suburb, with no one around.

What skills did I have, anyway? Olin hadn't prepared us for the job market. It was a college prep school, not a life prep school. We learned how to conquer dyslexia, or at least gain the upper hand on it, but like many high schools, practical skills were left in the shadows.

Explanations about career paths? Virtually nonexistent. Conversations about navigating life's path, even through its inevitable end? Barely a whisper. It all felt like a distant world. We were expected to find answers on our own—that's assuming we even knew enough to ask the right questions. Olin's focus was clear: build a bridge over dyslexia and get us to the other side. But once we crossed, the rest of life loomed ahead. For me, I was left wondering how to get life in focus.

It was my mother, once again, who helped me find work. She had been working for a real estate company that managed apartment complexes, and through her, I got a job at one.

At the apartment complex, I painted, hauled trash, and cleaned out incinerators. It wasn't so bad. There was a group of four to six high school guys working there, and they were pretty crazy.

One guy was a real motorhead. He had a 1955 Chevy in various stages of being rebuilt—a beast of a car with no paint, just a flat, dark gray primer that gave it a menacing, unfinished look. But under the hood, everything was pristine. The engine rumbled with a low, steady growl, its power vibrating through the pavement whenever he revved it.

That summer, I carpooled with the guys for a month. Motorhead loved showing off, weaving through traffic with reckless confidence, gunning it at green lights just to hear the tires screech. I often found myself wedged in the middle of the back seat, clutching whatever I could, unable to see much beyond the heads and shoulders in front of me. It felt like living in *American Graffiti*—these guys were walking clichés straight out of the movie, all swagger and adrenaline.

One day, on the way home from work, the usual rumble of the Chevy's engine was drowned out by shouting. The guys by the windows were leaning out, yelling at the car next to us. Their voices crackled with excitement, their bodies tense.

"Got a tire iron?" one of them asked, rummaging frantically through the backseat.

I froze, trying to process what was happening. It had all escalated so fast.

"Okay, next light," someone muttered, a wicked grin spreading across his face.

I stretch my neck, straining for a glimpse of the other car, I can only assume it was another car packed with just as many rowdy teenagers. My stomach tightened as we pulled up to the next red light.

Suddenly, the doors flew open.

The guys in our car jumped out, and so did the ones from the other. I couldn't see what was going on, but the air buzzed with tension. The scuffle was short-lived—more of a messy, frenzied clash than a real fight. Less than thirty seconds later, it was over. As quickly as it had started, it ended. The light turned green, and everyone scrambled back into their cars, breathless and laughing like they had just won some pointless prize.

"Man, did you see that? I got him right in the ribs with the jack handle!" one guy bragged, wiping a streak of blood from his knuckle. Another grinned, proudly showing off a torn sleeve and a small cut like it was a badge of honor.

I sat there in silence, trying to piece the events together. My heart pounded in my chest.

I never carpooled with them again.

I had a goal to buy a camera that summer. I saved every dollar from my paychecks and spent hours at the camera store, checking out different models. The Nikon FM was the professional's choice, not some fragile hobbyist camera, but it was expensive. I was also drawn to the Olympus OM1 because of its smaller size but seemed equally professional. Maybe, deep down, I imagined myself climbing mountains or backpacking in the wilderness.

I picked up a second job at Lawson's, a convenience store near the apartments. It was a lot like a 7-Eleven. The best part of the job was the variety of people who came in—real characters. I rang up sales, stocked shelves, and cleaned, counting every dollar I earned toward my goal.

Finally, toward the end of the summer, I had enough to buy the Olympus OM1, along with a flash. I walked into the camera store with $180 in ones, tens, and maybe a couple of twenties stuffed in my pockets. The look on the clerk's face as I pulled out the crumpled bills from my pockets was priceless. It was the highlight of my summer, aside from receiving that letter from Olin confirming my graduation.

By the end of October, the job at Lawson's was losing its appeal. Everyone my age was off at college, and I didn't want to be alone. I wanted to be around people my age.

One day, Grandpa said, "Jim, would you like to join me tomorrow? I have a meeting at Ashland College. You can tour the campus, and we'll have lunch afterward."

"Sure."

Grandpa was likable, with the kind of honor and sharp judgment of character you'd expect from a lawyer. I admired that about him — though, as his grandchild, I was probably a little biased.

At Ashland College I toured the campus, and we had lunch. Afterward, Grandpa took me to his old fraternity. No doubt, this was a carefully arranged covert mission by my mother.

Before I knew it, I was enrolled for the spring semester. They had a Radio & TV curriculum, and the idea of studying television thrilled me.

College started off great. A classmate from Olin was there and suggested I request a room on the 7th floor of Kem Hall, where he lived. Kem was a men's-only dorm, just a beer bottle's throw from the dining hall — a real advantage in the winter.

I arrived at my new dorm to find my roommate, Barry, staring out the window, his elbows on the sill, propping up his head. He was either bored or wondering what he was doing there. We got along great. We even had Economics together and would get stoned before class. We almost missed our final exam because we were too busy getting into the right frame of mind.

The 7th floor was definitely the stoner floor, though we didn't call it that. We played a lot of backgammon. It was fascinating — the game was like life. Some people only have one way to play it, relying on the roll of the dice. You can have a strategy, but if the dice don't give you the right roll, you're S.O.L. Some people played to get all their men around the board as quickly as possible. Others built defenses to block opponents. It was a fast, aggressive game, and the key was sticking to your strategy and not overthinking it.

The bong was the method of choice. We'd pass it around while playing backgammon. The loser had to take a hit. But the goal wasn't to get stoned— getting stoned was frowned upon. We smoked moderately, at least during that first semester. By the second semester, though, a newer generation moved in, and their goal was to get as stoned as possible. They'd even throw a game just to take a hit.

I was invited to pledge at Grandpa's fraternity, but I declined. I was too independent to subject myself to the conformity of personalities and peer pressure I perceived a fraternity involved. Still, through my time playing on the college lacrosse team, I got to know many of the fraternity brothers. They were all cool guys.

I watched plenty of the public pledging events. The college didn't have co-ed dorms, but my window overlooked the girls' dorm. Often, a group of frat pledges would gather out front, singing or shouting. For me, it was more annoying than entertaining, but it was also intriguing—it was campus life.

I thought the singing and shouting might be a covert way to strengthen their 'manly' voices. After all, how else do you learn to project your voice publicly? I'd seen girls do something similar— screaming and yelling at parties or on weekends. Maybe it was a social thing, maybe it was about deepening their voices. A deep voice carries a certain weight. A high-pitched voice just doesn't seem as credible. But, as with anything, taking it to the extreme loses its purpose.

Despite being at college, I still didn't quite fit in. I looked several years younger than I was. The guys with big bravados didn't take me seriously, and a few were bold or drunk enough to let me know it. But I took their comments, filed them away, and let them go. It's hard to be insulted when you don't accept the insult.

The seventh floor had its own group dynamic. We generally got along with everyone, whether it was sports or classes. I felt comfortable enough that one day I added a comment to the bathroom wall. The bathroom stalls were a place to compose—some comments were clever, current, even profound. Of course, they were all anonymous. I added my own, but soon regretted it.

One of the guys came out of the bathroom, loudly mocking a misspelled word, pointing out how it made no sense. I immediately knew it was mine and kept my mouth shut. So much for my bathroom publications.

A lot of freshmen were new to living away from home, but I didn't feel green. I had been living at a boarding school for the last four years. The biggest difference between high school and college for me was the presence of girls. They were everywhere, and it seemed like most guys had a girlfriend or were between relationships. Girls were interesting to observe, especially since I hadn't been around them since eighth grade.

There were two groups of girls who, for some reason, invited me to hang out from time to time. I can't say I spent more time with them than with the guys, but I usually had my eye on one of them, probably trying to get to know her better. What struck me as odd was how each group would badmouth the other, not realizing I was friends with both. I never pointed it out, just listened, amused by the divide.

My acne hadn't improved much since high school, but worse than that, I still looked five to eight years younger than I was. Deep down, I knew I wasn't a viable option for the college women. These were mature women looking for equally mature men, not some guy who looked like a freshman in high school.

College was where you got to pretend to be an adult for the first time—making your own decisions, dining in restaurants with a hip flair, and acting like your parents weren't paying for it all.

I wasn't shy about talking to girls, but getting them into bed was a mystery. Most of the girls interested in me were younger and seemed to want to play house. Were they as horny as I was? Did they want sex?

It always came back to the same issue—after sex, you had to talk to the person beside you. That almost always stopped me from pursuing relationships. Either I wasn't physically attracted, or we couldn't connect beyond the surface.

One night, a girl and I needed to get into the science building to study for an exam the next day. We arrived just as security was locking the doors.

"The building's closed for the night," the guard told us.

I looked at my friend and said, "There goes our exam scores."

Hearing my innocent comment, the guard was sympathetic and let us in—as long as we made sure to lock the door behind us.

Once inside, the girl turned to me, impressed.

"Way to go! That was great!" she said, as if I had planned it all.

It was just dumb luck.

My first semester of college turned out great. I had a cool roommate, did well in my classes, played lacrosse, and hung out with kids my age. Compared to Olin, I was having a blast. But like most freshmen, my second semester was a 180-degree turn.

Although most of my classmates were starting their sophomore year, I was still a freshman. Barry had moved to another dorm, and I didn't have much in common with my new roommate. Where he and I had played backgammon and taken hits, my new roommate only wanted to watch TV.

Everyone else was more serious about their studies, and I lost my connection with the guys I'd hung out with the previous semester. My interactions dwindled, and my studies became more challenging for several reasons.

I still wanted to study Radio & TV—it felt like a continuation of my AV experiences from Boulevard and junior high. I was excited about the idea of a career in broadcasting. A well-known Cleveland weatherman, had gone to Ashland, and that inspired me. But there was a shadow looming over my future.

The Radio & TV major was in the School of Arts, which required a foreign language to graduate. For someone with dyslexia, English was already as foreign as I could handle. The school pointed out the language requirement several times.

"Jim, you'll need to study a foreign language if you want to pursue Radio & TV," the college advisor told me.

My other option was business, which oddly didn't require a language. So, that fall, I took an accounting class, French, and a couple of Radio & TV classes.

I had a great time with my Radio & TV classes. I even started floor directing for the college's evening news. We all had a good laugh the first time I had to count down using my fingers—I completely screwed up. My fingers didn't seem to cooperate as I tried to fold each one into a fist during the countdown.

When I started the *Introduction to Multimedia* class, I knew I had made the right decision by attending Ashland. It was fantastic. The class helped me recall everything I had absorbed from my countless hours in front of the TV as a child. We covered everything from general programming to the early history of radio and TV, and even how an hour of television was meticulously structured to accommodate advertising.

The advertising section fascinated me, especially the breakdown of time slots. A standard hour of television wasn't really an hour of content—it was closer to 42 or 45 minutes, with the rest reserved for commercials. Those commercial slots were divided into precise increments: one-minute ads, 30-second spots, 15-second quick hits, and even 10-second blips. The shorter the ad, the more information it had to cram into an impossibly small window.

"How long is one second?" the instructor asked.

I knew the answer instinctively. I had done timed exercises in elementary school, where I had to recall a string of seven numbers flashed in just 1/15th of a second. I had also developed a sense of fractions of a second through my 35mm SLR camera—one second of exposure was an eternity in photography.

"Think about how much your brain absorbs in a blink," the instructor continued. "Now imagine compressing an entire advertisement into that space."

Time was money. Once we understood the minimum exposure required for a message to register in our minds, advertisers could justify shorter ads, cram more spots into a broadcast, and maximize revenue. The real trick was how efficiently our brains processed images. Even with ad cuts lasting less than a second, we still absorbed the message. It was a revelation—watching the way media had evolved, adapting to the limits of human perception while shaping consumer behavior at the same time.

Accounting, on the other hand, was a struggle. We had to use paper ledgers, and while I understood the math, the credit-debit system was beyond me. I couldn't grasp why it was necessary, and no matter how hard I tried, I just couldn't get it. Even with a fraternity buddy trying to help me, my mind strained but came up empty.

French was even worse—it felt like reliving my struggle with English all over again. At Olin, it had taken four grueling years of Reading classes just to get a solid grasp of spelling and reading in my own language. So, when I faced French, the same roadblocks appeared—letter pairs that made no sense, sound combinations that seemed impossible to predict. The professors assumed we all had a basic understanding of how language worked, but I didn't. No one explained the fundamentals of French that I had fought so hard to master in English. Without that foundation, I was completely lost—and I flunked.

By the end of my second semester, the administration sat me down.

"Jim, we're sorry, but you don't have the requirements to stay in the School of Arts. We need to give priority to those who do."

"Hey, I'm dyslexic," I said, as if they understood what that meant. "Do you have any idea what it took for me to learn to read and spell? French feels exactly the same."

"Sorry," they replied. "What we can do is allow you to take a photography class while you work on your French. Pass French, and we'll see about getting you back into the School of Arts. But in the meantime, we'll move you to the School of Business."

Photography was something I loved, so I agreed. But when I returned after winter break, I found out the photography class was full—I wasn't in it. I felt betrayed. That class was the only reason I had stayed. I didn't want to study business—it didn't interest me in the slightest.

In a rare moment of clarity, I thought, *I'm paying to be here. If I can't take the classes I want, why waste the money?*

That was it. I withdrew from all my classes in the first week and packed up my things.

In hindsight, there are moments in life that turn out to be pivotal, and not being able to major in Radio & TV was one of them. If I'd been able to, I likely would have pursued a career in television and never looked back. It could have provided a traditional life and career path. I could see myself staying in TV—maybe becoming a director, or even a cinematographer.

It was 1977, and I would have graduated in the early 1980s—just in time for the explosion of cable TV. But the foreign language requirement derailed that path and set me on a course far from the mainstream. Knowing I couldn't meet that requirement put me on a journey that led, at age 21, to the second and most profound life-changing event that shaped my beliefs and attitude toward life.

Order, Order, Order

After leaving Ashland, I worked at Brandywine, a local Cleveland ski area where I had been taking ski instructor lessons during that fall. I had been hired as a ski instructor for afternoon school groups, mostly junior high kids who had no interest in lessons and just wanted to have fun.

Keeping their attention, let alone teaching them anything, was a struggle. My chaotic classes must have been obvious because soon enough, I was offered a job on the night snow crew instead. I didn't complain—it paid better, and I had nothing better to do anyway.

The night snow crew was responsible for making snow and grooming the slopes. I even got to drive the snow cats, which was pretty cool. My main task, however, was walking to each snowmaking machine on the hill and clearing the built-up ice from the nozzles.

It was a cold, wet job. I wore layers of long underwear, jeans, ski pants, thermal shirts, a down vest, and a long coat. But I quickly learned that the snow guns soaked you in wet snow, so I bought a yellow rain suit to wear over everything. By the end of the season, the yellow had turned a greasy gray, and I had to use duct tape to patch the seams that split open from the cold.

The winter was brutal in the Cleveland area that year. We had record breaking snowstorms. One storm was so bad that semis were buried in snowdrifts. The next morning, you could only see their antennas poking through the snow.

I worked from 11 p.m. to 11 a.m. and had to drive in those conditions every night. The TV weather reports often told people to stay home because all the roads were closed, but I didn't have that option. The news made it sound like the roads were completely impassable, but in reality, the interstates were open— snow-covered, but still drivable.

That winter gave me plenty of time to think. Walking up the hill to each snow gun, I had hours to reflect on where my life was heading. The scene was like something out of an old black-and-white movie— the sky was pitch black, and the snow-covered ground was stark white. It was ironic that I was so interested in photography, and now, every night, I was living in a black-and-white world on the ski hill.

The frost-covered branches stretched like lace across the black horizon. Standing on top of the hill, I could look down at the maintenance barn, its doors framed by a small pool of light. From up there, that light seemed tiny, almost insignificant. But when I stood in it, the glow was blinding, and I couldn't see beyond it.

It struck me then: light can confine your view, narrowing it to only what it illuminates. But in the darkness, your perspective opens up, free from the boundaries of artificial light. The snow, glowing faintly in the night, became both a canvas and a void, shifting the way I saw everything around me.

One night, I saw an orange moon, and I couldn't help but think of the cover of Neil Young's *Harvest* album. Neil Young's music had been a big part of my life back then.

I've been first and last
Look at how the time goes past.
But I'm all alone at last,
Rolling home to you.
Old man, take a look at my life,
I'm a lot like you.

Working on the snow crew was fine, even with the 12-hour long shifts. It was hard to complain when you got to drive snow cats. But by the end of March, after three months of night work, I found myself dozing off during idle moments. The ski season was winding down, and they gave me the option to quit with my full bonus. So, I did.

It was April, and I had to find another job. The winter had given me time to reflect, though I couldn't say it pointed me in any clear direction. My desire to pursue photography was still there, but not in the conventional sense. I didn't dream of being a "photographer," and I didn't even know you could make a living at it. Reflecting back now, I think what I wanted was to explore life visually, to see and capture it without the pressure of making it a profession. Photography felt like a personal lens on the world rather than a job title I could wear. But at that time, all I really knew was that I needed money to survive.

During the winter, I had been living at Dad's apartment while my older brother was away at college. But with him coming home for the summer, I moved back to Mom's house. Besides, Mom's house had a darkroom under the basement stairs, which felt like the perfect setup for someone getting into photography.

Dad reminded me that I needed to help cover the cost of food and housing, which gave me a sense of responsibility for paying my way. It also gave me a feeling of contributing to the family, something that I think is often undervalued. For me, it was a good thing. Slowly, I started to see my self-worth improve. I had an active role in my own life—paying for my living.

That spring, I took a job at a restaurant, relying on the skills I'd picked up during past summers. It was a night job, which meant I had my days open to pursue photography. My first gig was at a spaghetti joint near the Lawson's I had worked at the previous summer. The dinner shift was perfect for my schedule.

With the money I'd saved from my snow crew job, I signed up for a beginner photography class at the Cleveland Institute of Art. That class was fascinating. I learned how to develop and print black-and-white film for the first time. I was introduced to dodging (holding back light from certain parts of the print) and burning (adding exposure to other parts), which were exciting techniques to use in refining the print.

Walking into the institute's six-person darkroom felt like entering a cool, hidden cave. It took a full minute for my eyes to adjust to the reddish-orange safety light. The smell of fixer and stop bath, the sound of running water—it was incredible. I felt at home.

For our final project, we had to present our best image. I chose to print a photograph of Grandpa's cottage, nestled deep in the forests. I needed to burn in the upper portion of the print where the trees were. It was near the end of class, and I was down to my last sheet of 11x14 photo paper.

As I made my final print, I pulled the paper from the easel and instantly realized I had messed up— I forgot to burn the trees. The easel hadn't moved, and I thought I could just place the paper back in the same spot and burn the trees as intended. Simple enough, I thought.

But when I watched the image develop in the tray, I noticed something unusual. The paper hadn't aligned perfectly in the easel, and the second exposure caused a slight misalignment of the trees, making them appear double-exposed. At first, I was disappointed, but then I realized something: the trees looked like they were moving. The double exposure added a sense of motion to the image that wasn't there before.

When I presented the photo to the class, they were all silent. Usually, the students and instructor had something to say about everyone's final print, but this time, the silence stretched on, creating an uneasy feeling in the room.

I like to think they were in awe. It was my first happy mistake—a printing error that made the photo far better than I could have planned. It wouldn't be my last. In fact, one of my future happy mistakes would end up changing the layout of a famous movie poster.

Around this time, for no particular reason, I started writing in the spiralbound notebook I had bought during my last semester of college. I'd used it the previous summer to record the rebuilding of my 1969 Mustang after I wrecked it. I'd even bought another '69 Mustang for parts while preparing the wrecked one for transplants.

College hadn't been for nothing—I found pages where I had set up 'debit' and 'credit' columns to track my money. The notebook became a place to journal my life and dreams, with no specific intention behind it. It was just a friendly space to record my thoughts.

Sometime in early summer, I sold the Mustang. I can't recall why exactly, other than it felt like the right thing to do. Maybe it symbolized the end of my college days, or perhaps I was entering a new phase in life without fully realizing it. I just knew that selling it felt like a natural progression.

Without a car, I walked to work at the spaghetti joint. I managed this for a few weeks but started looking for something more challenging. Oddly, not long after I sold the Mustang—just when I was getting tired of walking home in the dark—I landed a broiler cook job at Don's Butcher Block, a steak and seafood restaurant just three blocks from my mother's house.

If you've ever worked in a restaurant, you know that being the broiler person is a decent position. It's a step up from washing dishes and light years ahead of bussing tables. I never even considered being a waiter—that just wasn't me.

My workspace at Don's was compact yet efficient, designed so everything I needed was within reach. Behind me was a large, two-drawer broiler, and to my left, an oven with massive gas grates, while a steamer for rice and veggies stood to my right. I worked at a one-foot-wide butcher-block counter, beneath it were coolers that held trays of meat and fish—monkfish, sole, stuffed sole, halibut, and scallops.

My process was simple: I'd ladle a wine-butter mixture over the fish, turn 180 degrees, and place them in the broiler behind me. The setup made for smooth, efficient work. Just to my right, in full view of customers, was a massive roast beef we carved into sixteen-ounce slabs. The coolers also held New York strips and T-bones, keeping everything ready for a busy night.

The rhythm of the evening quickly fell into place. Waiters and waitresses would call out, "Order!" and impale the tickets on a large needle holder in front of me. I'd clip the orders on a wire above my workstation, reading them and sliding them down to the plater.

All night, the music of the kitchen played out like this: "Order!" *Sheeeeee*— the sound of the ticket being impaled. Grab the order, read it, and place the steaks and fish where I knew the broiler would cook them properly—well-done in the hottest spots, medium or rare in the cooler areas. There were no timers, just instinct and experience.

Reflecting now, I think being on the spectrum with some ADHD might have been a hidden advantage here. My concentration was running full throttle, processing each order and tracking every detail to keep things straight in my mind.

At first, I'd have a moment or two between orders, but as the night wore on, the pace, and heat from the boilers picked up, and so did my intake of ice-cold Sprite—sugar water to cool off and keep my energy up. I'd easily down two or three gallons each night, which left me wired, making it nearly impossible to fall asleep once the night was over.

"Order!" Sheeeeee. Grab the order: New York medium, filet rare, stuffed sole. I'd take a step, grab a fish, put it in a pie pan, ladle on the wine and butter, and pop them on the broiler.

Then things would escalate: "Order! Order!" Sheeeee, sheeeee. The orders stacked up. Cod, sole, someone wanted a scallop casino— chopped herbs, peppers, onions, breadcrumbs, butter—into the broiler it went.

"Order! Order! Order!" The pace picked up. I'd just plated one order, and suddenly there were twenty more waiting. The kitchen became a blur of orders, broiling steaks, and frying fish.

"Order, order, order, order!" Now ten more orders. I'd barely gotten rid of five, and I was running on sugar water and adrenaline. The rare steaks from the earlier orders were ready since they took less time, but the rest? It was chaos. I was in the zone—pushing out orders as fast as I could, rarely having a moment to think.

After two months of this, I started talking out loud to blow off some of the pressure, and the relentless pace was wearing on me. The rush had been fun at first, but eventually, you reach your limit.

One night, the manager had to step in for the front plater—the person who adds the veggies and checks that each order is complete before it goes to the table. He was trying to keep up, but I could see the plates piling up as he struggled to plate the endless string of orders. I heard the familiar cries of "Order! Order!" and watched the chaos unfold.

The manager turned to me, a dazed look in his eyes, and said, "Am I going too fast for you?"

Without missing a beat, I replied, "No," too focused on getting the orders cooked to think beyond the literal meaning of his words.

It wasn't until later that it hit me—maybe what he really meant was, "I can't keep up."

Picking up on implied meaning has never been my strong suit. Maybe it's the spectrum, but processing undertones and unspoken cues often feels like trying to solve a riddle without all the pieces. I could easily misinterpret it, so I've learned to brush it off. If someone can't say what they mean directly, I figure that's on them. So I just kept pushing out food, grinning at the absurdity of it all while he scrambled to keep pace.

My photography class at CIA was going great. Without a car, I took the bus down to University Circle, which gave me a chance to walk around the lagoon in front of the art museum—something I wouldn't have done if I'd been driving.

I was lucky that it was a straight shot down Mayfield Road for about ten miles. I probably would've been lost if I'd needed to transfer buses. Riding the city bus was an interesting experience—not quite like Greyhound, but the people riding it definitely reminded me of those you'd see at a Greyhound bus station.

Although the bus worked for the time being, it was getting old fast. I'd saved some money and started looking for my next used car. It was the end of summer, and my younger brother and I were spending time together. He helped me look for a new ride. For some reason, a Volkswagen appealed to me.

We found an oxidized red 1968 VW Fastback being sold by a laid-back, hippy-ish girl. She seemed happy that I was buying it. The VW was cool—disc brakes, fuel injection, engine in the back, spare tire in the front. All features unheard of in American cars from the same year. I loved the sound of the fuel pump kicking in when I turned the key.

That September, there were three concerts I couldn't miss: Yes, Neil Young, and Jethro Tull. (Can't relate? Swap in the bands that shaped your own soundtrack.) Without a day job, I had the luxury of getting up at the crack of dawn to snag tickets.

As it turned out, I was a little *too* eager. In the 1970s, concert tickets were sold at record stores, and I showed up at 5:00 AM—two hours before anyone else, and four hours before the tickets went on sale. I sat alone in front of the store, watching the wind blow discarded paper across the empty parking lot.

Out of nowhere, two cop cars came speeding in, from different directions, and did circles around each other. Maybe it was some kind of pursuit exercise, but to me, it just looked like they were goofing off. The wait was worth it—I scored front-row seats!

It was the week of September 18th. My brother and I went to see Yes on Wednesday—our second time seeing them live. The Neil Young concert was 9 days later on Friday, but the restaurant suddenly informed me I couldn't take the night off. I was puzzled.

They required two weeks' notice for time off, and I had submitted my requests for all three concert dates three weeks in advance. Now they were telling me no? This was Neil Young. *Front-row seats!* I remember thinking, *screw it, I'm going.*

I had only gotten my VW a few weeks before, and having a car again made me feel free. Driving down I-71 toward the Richfield Coliseum, I noticed other concert-goers in the lane next to me. They motioned to me that they had a joint and wanted to share.

"Okay, pass it over," I said.

Here I was, driving 50 mph, passing a joint between cars on the highway. The adventure had begun.

The concert was everything I had hoped for and more. Neil Young opened with an acoustic set, starting with *Sugar Mountain*, a song about being 20—my age at the time—and my darkroom was under the stairs at Mom's.

Now you're underneath the stairs
And you're givin' back some glares

...
You can't be twenty on Sugar Mountain
Though you're thinking that you're leavin' there too soon...

Then came *I Am a Child*:
I am a child, I'll last a while.
You can't conceive of the pleasure in my smile.

In the second set, Crazy Horse took the stage, and that's when things got serious. The stage revealed massive twenty-foot speakers, and they tore into the kind of raw, powerful rock that only Neil Young and Crazy Horse could deliver.

The show ended with *Tonight's the Night*, and those words took on a whole new meaning for me that night.

The next night, I went into the restaurant. They reprimanded me for taking the night off without permission and fired me on the spot. Then, in the same breath, they told me to take a week off and come back if I'd learned my lesson.

I was confused. Were they really punishing me? They must have thought I'd feel bad about not working. Sure, I missed the money, but not the work. *Order, order, order!*

After a day of thinking it over, I realized something: I didn't like restaurant work. College hadn't worked out either, thanks to that foreign language requirement. But somewhere in the middle of all that frustration, a light bulb went off. *I'm free to do whatever I want. Why put up with this if there's no real benefit?*

That night, I made up my mind: I'm getting out of here. What do I really want to do? I wanted to live my childhood dream. I wanted to live in the Rockies.

I wrote "Seven Week Save" in my notebook and added new comments each day, capturing fresh thoughts as they came.

Save money by not spending it.
Sell stuff.

Spend only on photography, food, and rent.
Write West Now
Your life can't wait
Be positive
Improve your skills
Take pride in what you do
Be productive
Relax
Work at your dreams & ambitions
Don't leave things for other people to do them
Show how you want to be treated
Be strong, physically as well as mentally
Lucky people Work on their luck
Luck can be worked for
Work for luck
Do it!
Go for it!

I read those lines almost every night as I prepared to leave. Every bit of my energy and thinking was focused on my goal—leaving and living in the Rockies.

I threw out all my old books, yearbooks, ribbons, and the clutter of childhood. I think my parents might have been a little concerned by the purging. In some ways, it might have looked like I was contemplating something drastic, like suicide. But that was far from my reality. I wasn't giving up; far from it. I was getting ready to start living the life I wanted.

For those last weeks, I worked at Don's without a care in the world. *Order, order, order* still echoed in my mind as I lay in bed, trying to sleep, but those thoughts quickly gave way to my plans for the road ahead. Should I visit my brothers at the colleges they were attending? Could I stay with my cousins in Boulder? Which route should I take—I-80 or I-70 across the country?

One of the last things I did before leaving was print my entry for the NOVA show—*My Brother and I*. A small but satisfying victory came when I learned it had been accepted. It was a final bit of validation before setting off into the unknown.

The last sweet justice at Don's came when I quit. I punched my timecard one final time and walked straight to the manager's office.

"Sir, everything's put away, my station's clean. Here's my last timecard. Send my final paycheck to my address—I won't be here tomorrow. I'm quitting."

I turned before he could sputter out a response, but not before I caught the flicker of shock on his face. That alone was satisfying.

Then, I was outside. The kitchen clatter and greasy heat evaporated behind me, replaced by the crisp night air. A wave of freedom hit— sharp, electric. I was done. Done with the noise, the chaos, the Order, Order, Order, and the heat of the broiler in that cramped space.

I walked to my VW, heart pounding, knowing that by tomorrow, I'd be heading for the mountains. It was thrilling and terrifying all at once, that moment when the roller coaster crests its first hill, the pause just before the drop. I let out a breath, gripping the door handle, ready for the ride ahead.

Steamboat

I was ahead of schedule—ready in just six weeks. I saved as much as I could, got the VW checked out, packed the essentials, and hit the road. I knew my destination: the mountains. Beyond that, I didn't know, and I didn't care. From my time working at the local ski hill, I knew big ski resorts out west always needed staff. Before leaving, I sent letters to a few places and got a response from one in Montana. That was all the direction I needed.

With a sheet thrown over my belongings in the back seat of the VW, I was ready to go. I might've said "Adios, Cleveland!" with the same confidence I'd have at 27, but this time—striking out on my own at 20—felt different. It wasn't about escaping; it was about the excitement of stepping into the unknown. In just eleven days, I'd turn 21 and be living a childhood dream.

I took I-71 south from Cleveland to Columbus, then continued southwest to Cincinnati, where I stopped to see my younger brother at his dorm. College wasn't his thing—he also struggled with the social dynamics and the unspoken hierarchy. Like me, he had always been adventurous, carving his own path, but he was far more outgoing—the extroverted version of me.

That evening, we went to a local bar to hear Tom Waits. After a few beers, as the night wound down, my brother suddenly disappeared. A while later, he reappeared near the exit, casually saying, "Yeah, I saw Tom Waits." I figured he'd tried to meet him but got bounced by security or something. That was the night.

The next morning, I set out for Purdue to visit my older brother. He was the opposite of my younger brother. After flunking out of college, he turned things around, went to community college, and eventually made it to Purdue, where he was thriving.

After catching up with him, I hit the road again, excitement growing with every mile. I passed through St. Louis and drove through the night, making the journey from Purdue to Boulder in one go.

When I saw the sign reading *Entering Colorful Colorado*, I was pumped. But with the sun already set, I wouldn't be able to see the mountains rise from the horizon. I still had three hours to go. I thought, *Go for it!* and kept driving. Around midnight—though it felt like 2 AM after such a long day—I finally rolled into Boulder.

From a convenience store, I called my cousin John for directions to his place. Exhausted, I got back in the car, only to realize a few blocks later that I'd left the handbrake on. The smell of something burning made me panic, thinking my car was breaking down. When I figured it out, I was too wiped out to care—I just wanted to get to my cousin's house.

The drive itself felt anticlimactic since I couldn't see the mountains in the dark. But stepping outside the next morning was like Dorothy arriving in Munchkin land. The mountains, the crisp air, the vibrant colors—it was all full-blown Technicolor. I had never felt so alive.

For the first time, I was completely in charge of my life. No school, no authority dictating my choices. I was surrounded by people my age, and for once, I felt like I belonged. This was where I was meant to be.

John and I drove up to Nederland, a small town nestled in the mountains northwest of Boulder, for lunch. The fresh air and towering pines gave the day a sense of adventure, a preview of what lay ahead.

When we returned, I realized it was time to gear up for the journey. I bought a tent, a warm down mummy bag, and a Coleman gas stove — essentials for life on the road, I told myself.

But those purchases put a bigger dent in my budget than I'd expected. As I stared at my dwindling funds, I shrugged it off. *Well, I need shelter, don't I?* I was making my own choices, learning as I went. Any reasonable person might have panicked at how little money I had left, but not me. I was young, driven, and confident nothing could derail my mission.

The next morning, as I packed up to leave, I asked John, "What's the shortest way to get to Vail?"

John smirked. "Do you want the shortest or the quickest?"

"Give me the shortest!"

It didn't take long to see what he meant. The shortest route was a winding road full of hairpin turns and steep switchbacks, but the views were stunning. I had picked Vail because it was a renowned ski resort, and I figured finding work there would be simple.

Driving along I-70 toward the Eisenhower Tunnel, my VW fastback groaned under the strain of the climb, slowing to a near crawl as cars zipped past me. But I didn't mind. I was grinning the whole way. When your car barely manages twenty miles per hour in second gear, you've got plenty of time to soak in the views — and I wasn't in a rush.

As I approached Vail, I glanced to my left and felt a twinge of disappointment. It looked more like a city than the mountain retreat I had envisioned — just buildings tightly packed into the narrow valley, leaving no open spaces to breathe. This wasn't the serene escape I'd been hoping for. I kept driving, turning north onto Route 131, aiming for Steamboat Springs. My plan was to pass through it on my way to Montana, where a ski job awaited.

The drive north was breathtaking. The landscape unfolded in a stark beauty, vast and slightly barren, but captivating in its own way. By the time I arrived in Steamboat, the sun had long since set. I remembered a KOA campground from a geology trip back in tenth grade, so I headed there, navigating by memory.

Pitch darkness greeted me as I set up my tent for the first time, fumbling with the unfamiliar parts. I managed to get it standing without resorting to the instructions, which I found the next day. The cold mountain air seeped in, and I crawled into my mummy bag, feeling the icy bite of the night.

Lying there in the dark, a deep realization began to settle in: I was truly on my own. It felt like taking my first steps as a child—wobbling between exhilaration and vulnerability. There was no one to catch me if I stumbled, no one to lean on. Every decision was mine to make, every direction mine to choose.

This wasn't the era of cell phones or the internet—no instant messages, no quick calls home. If I wanted to reach someone, it meant writing a letter and waiting weeks for a reply, or making an expensive long-distance call I couldn't afford. My car didn't have an address, and neither did I. Too far from home and too broke to turn back, I was bound only by the horizon.

Yet, instead of fear, I felt an overwhelming sense of belonging, something I hadn't experienced since my days at Red Raider Camp. The world seemed simpler, a place where I could just be. This was different, but that same quiet comfort returned: I was where I was supposed to be.

The morning air was crisp and biting, but my mummy bag had done its job. I slipped on my jacket and stepped outside, greeted by the sun's warmth cutting through the chill. Its golden rays mirrored the smile on my face.

On the way to the bathhouse, I noticed my VW, covered in a heavy frost, standing ready for another day of adventure. After washing up, I fired up the Coleman stove, boiled water, and filled my stainless-steel thermos with a mix of coffee and hot chocolate—a comforting ritual I'd picked up during my nights at Brandywine. The road ahead felt promising, and so did the day.

Next, I packed up my tent and prepared to check out the job market in Steamboat before heading north through Wyoming to Jackson Hole and then Montana. Sliding into the driver's seat, I turned the key, listening for the familiar sound of the fuel pump activating. I cranked the engine, but it didn't start.

"Shit," I muttered, trying it again. Still nothing.

As I sat there, a guy strolled by, sizing up the situation immediately. "Fuel line freeze-up, eh?"

"Is that so?" I asked, feeling unsure but hopeful.

"Yep, pretty common around here. Just give it some time. The sun'll thaw it out."

"Thanks," I replied, a mix of frustration and resignation settling in.

I climbed onto the picnic table, letting the sun warm my back as I waited. The nearby stream gurgled softly, and I took in the snow-dusted mountains surrounding me.

By 10:00 AM, the frost had melted, and the car finally roared to life. Relieved, I drove into town and stopped at the first gas station I saw. I picked up a bottle of Heet, a gas additive meant to clear water from the fuel line, and poured it in, feeling cautiously optimistic.

Just as I was about to leave, I noticed something dripping beneath the car. "Damn," I muttered, crouching down to inspect it. A quick swipe of my finger confirmed it—gas. The frozen water had caused a small crack in the fuel line. I knew it was only a matter of time before it got worse.

In that moment, my plans for Montana vanished. The car needed fixing, and I needed work—fast. It was decided: Steamboat became my final destination, whether I liked it or not.

I drove up to the ski slopes, which were separated from town by a two-lane road. Construction was everywhere—new condos rising up on all sides. The older part of the resort, Ski Time Square, had a quieter vibe, and I took it all in before heading back into town.

On the way back, I picked up a hitchhiker who assured me there were plenty of jobs around. It felt like a good omen. After wandering through town and picking up some groceries—mostly canned food—I returned to the KOA. With money running low, I paid for eight days at the campsite, leaving myself just twenty dollars.

I found a spot near the stream, pitched my tent, and made it my base. The weather was turning colder, and snow seemed imminent. I wasn't sure how long I'd be staying, so I chose a small group of trees to block the wind and set up a picnic table on its side for extra shelter.

That evening, I fired up the Coleman stove, heated some beans and franks, and boiled water for my thermos. After dinner, I sat in the VW, smoked a bowl, and absorbed the quiet. No TV, no radio—just the rustling of wind through the trees and the soft gurgle of the stream. The sky faded from deep blue to black as I read through my notebook and scribbled a few lines:

So you're in Steamboat Springs.
Now what?
Get a job, any job.

Mostly, I just sat with myself. The stillness felt grounding, the kind of silence that calms restless thoughts. When the cold eventually drove me to my tent, I crawled inside and slept soundly, the crisp mountain air pressing against my little shelter.

The next morning mirrored the first—cold air greeted me, but the sun's warmth soon cut through the chill. The stream babbled just yards from my tent, its steady rhythm providing a peaceful backdrop to the stillness of the campsite.

I savored the slow process of waking up, enjoying the simple act of firing up the stove and waiting for the water to boil. There was no rush. The landscape, even with its bare trees and late-autumn chill, felt serene—a quiet prelude to the coming snow.

After packing up my "kitchen" and stowing everything back in the VW, I decided to check out the Ramada Inn I'd noticed the day before. Being part of a well-known hotel chain, I figured it would have a restaurant—and maybe a job for me. The manager, Steve, wasn't in, but the hostess handed me an application and told me to come back the next day.

Feeling confident that I'd land the job, I stopped my search and decided to explore the area.

Later, back at the KOA after a drive up to Rabbit Ears Pass, I realized just how deserted the campground was. Who camps in November, especially during the week? The sky was dazzlingly clear, a stark contrast to Cleveland's perpetual gray. I sat by the stream, pipe in hand, watching the day slip by. The cool air mingled with the sun's warmth, creating a perfect balance.

The stream had become my companion, its presence constant—there when I went to sleep and there when I woke. Watching leaves and twigs drift along its current, I felt a quiet reminder of life's ceaseless flow. Time never pauses; like the stream, life moves forward, carrying us with it.

As evening settled in, I gathered sticks and branches for a small fire. The warmth was fleeting, but it gave me a task—something grounding in the encroaching darkness.

Later, I sat in the VW, writing by flashlight, careful not to drain the car battery. It was only 7:30, but the sun had long since dipped below the horizon, and the cold pressed in, sharp and biting.

I switched off the flashlight to let my gaze wander beyond the confines of the VW, staring at the moon. Its glow cast silvery shadows across the barren trees, a quiet reminder of how small I was in this vast wilderness. Turning the light back on, I wrote:

Moonlight

Wildnessssssss

The cold crept further in, and the VW's broken heater offered no reprieve. Besides, starting the engine would have broken the sacred silence of the night. I thought about the fire, how it constantly needed more wood to stay alive—a simple yet profound reminder that everything in life requires fuel, including me.

To keep warm

Feed the fire

Food is the fuel

Movement caught my eye at the neighboring campsite. A VW microbus had pulled in, and a guy stepped out, stretching as he surveyed the quiet site. He walked over and introduced himself.

"Lynn and I just drove down from Minnesota. We're spending the winter skiing. Name's Jimmy. If the president can be called Jimmy, I figure I can too."

I laughed. "Funny, I'm Jim."

We chatted for a while, exchanging stories and plans. Before heading back to his van, Jimmy suggested we hang out the next day after my meeting at the Ramada.

The following morning, I met with Steve, the hiring manager. His laid-back demeanor mirrored the town's vibe—he was a skier, content to be far from the city.

"I see you worked at two restaurants this year. How was it being the broiler person?" he asked.

"Hot and fast-paced, but I liked it." I did, though the pace could get to me.

"Where are you living? The KOA?"

"I just got into town. It works—they have hot showers, and I'm looking for a more permanent place. If you're wondering, I have a wind-up alarm clock."

Satisfied, he offered me the morning shift, 6:00 AM to 2:00 PM.

That evening, I met up with Jimmy and Lynn at the Cameo, a local pub buzzing with energy. The place was packed with construction workers and locals, their voices rising in a collective hum as they talked excitedly about the upcoming ski season. Over beers, Jimmy and Lynn mentioned they had found a condo and needed one more person.

"You in?" Jimmy asked with a grin.

How great this adventure had become.

The next morning marked my twenty-first birthday—the official start of my twenty-second year on this planet. Feeling a quiet pride, I walked into the nearest liquor store, ready to embrace the moment. The bell above the door jingled as I stepped in, the faint smell of old wood and cigarette smoke lingering in the air.

Before I could say anything, the lady behind the counter, with her sharp eyes and no-nonsense attitude, gave me a hard look and barked, "You're too young to be in here!" She hadn't even checked my ID—just made a snap judgment based on my face.

Irritated but amused, I shot her a look and pulled out my ID. "Aw, come on," I said, holding it up for her to see.

Her stern demeanor quickly softened as she realized her mistake, the corners of her mouth twitching into an awkward smile.

It was Saturday night, and I still had three nights left at the KOA campground. Just ten days ago, I had left Cleveland, visited my brothers, seen my cousins in Boulder, and now here I was in Steamboat Springs.

I'd paid for eight days at the campground and was down to my last $15. The future was uncertain, but that's exactly what I had craved — to step into the unknown. I had prepared as best I could. Maybe I'd spent too much on the tent and sleeping bag, but they were essentials, keeping me warm and sheltered.

The week had been kind to me. I landed a job at the Ramada Inn as a morning and noon line cook. The job provided meals and would soon provide a paycheck. Housing had also resolved itself with little effort. Jim and Lynn had left the KOA to stay with Steve and Darcy until our condo was ready in two weeks. Everything was falling into place, and I couldn't believe my luck.

After finishing my dinner of beans and franks, I heated water for my usual coffee-and-cocoa mix. The creek babbled just feet from my picnic table, and the fire beside me crackled, keeping the night's chill at bay. Overhead, the stars pierced a deep indigo sky, with wisps of clouds hinting at the snow to come.

I grabbed a beer chilling in the stream — my makeshift cooler — and twisted off the cap. My birthday party was a simple affair, yet it felt profound. I pulled out my pipe, lit a bowl, and took a slow, deep toke. As I exhaled, watching the smoke rise into the crisp mountain air and dissolve into the darkness. I stared into the flames, their flicker hypnotic, and reached for my notebook.

Place: KOA outside of Steamboat Springs
Time: 7:00pm
Event: My Birthday
I'm sitting by a fire in a KOA writing this to say
I'm 21 and oh what fun
Making my life the way I want it to be
I have been dreaming about living in the Rockies but now the dream is a
reality.

I grabbed another beer from the stream, cracked it open, and glanced around. The cold bit harder the farther I stepped from the fire. Tossing a few more logs onto the flames, I settled back onto the picnic table. Taking a drag from the pipe, I cupped it in my hands, savoring its warmth against the chill.

Time: 7:55
Nice night.
Fire is doing fine.
Heard cars & trucks on Rt. 40 cruising along.
The smoke is coming this way, and is here. I must move now.

So I stood up and moved to pull another cold one from the stream and threw a few more pieces of wood into the flames, saving the rest for tomorrow. The firelight flickered against the trees as I stood, gazing at the embers. The solitude didn't feel lonely; it felt expansive, like the mountains themselves.

Time: 9:04
Fire is dying out.
The clouds are rolling in.
I'm turning in with the lights all out.

* * *

Let me pause here: as I reread my journal and strive to be honest, I can't ignore how much "recreational" pot I smoked back then. It was the late 1970s, and pot was as common on college campuses as Frisbees and bell-bottoms. What we had wasn't nearly as potent as today's legal marijuana. Nowadays, it's all about the bud, but in the 70s finding any bud in a nickel or dime bag felt like striking gold. Most of the time, it was just leaves, offering a much mellower high.

Over the years, I've learned about medications for ADHD, autism, and behaviors society often tries to "quiet." Ironically, some of the most creative and revolutionary ideas have come from individuals like us. I wonder if pot played that role for me - to calm my mind, much like these medications are designed to do for others.

* * *

The next day, winter made its first real appearance—it started to snow. By Tuesday, my last paid day at the KOA, the weather had turned into a slushy mix of snow and rain. It was cold, and with only $15 to my name, I was cutting it close. My paycheck from the Ramada would arrive on Friday, but until then, I relied on the free breakfast and lunch at work. Dinner, however, was scarce.

After my shift, I met up with Jim, Lynn, Steve, Darcy, and a new face—Bob. Bob had a room at a place called the Haystack, and thankfully, he offered me a spare bed for a few nights. While staying with him, Bob introduced me to a book that left a lasting impression: *Inner Skiing* by Timothy Gallwey and Bob Kriegel.

"It's the best book about skiing I've ever read," Bob said, handing it to me.

Intrigued, I began reading, and soon I couldn't put it down. The book explored quieting the mind and trusting the body's natural abilities. It described the mental games people play, especially in sports like tennis, but with skiing, your only opponent is yourself. The internal chatter—critique of every turn, doubt, hesitation—all worked against you.

One concept that resonated deeply was the idea of "Self 1" and "Self 2." *Self 1* was the tense, critical part, full of fear, hesitation, and expectations. *Self 2* was the opposite—free, smooth, relaxed, and rhythmic. Fascinated, I copied these lists into my notebook to keep the contrast clear.

Throughout the winter, I often returned to those lists. I stopped focusing on *Self 1* and embraced *Self 2*, even darkening the *Self 2* words in my notebook, emphasizing their energy. I'd say them to myself as I skied—"free, smooth, speed, rhythmic, flowing"—feeling and embodying each word. The fear of falling, the mental barriers that held me back, faded as I internalized the lessons.

On the same page, I wrote, "Increase Your Awareness (IYA)" and "To aim for less is to fall short of realizing the most important potential each of us possesses."

I even copied the quote from Guru Maharaji that appeared in the book:

"Desire is like a force. One force is generated by mind, and one is generated naturally within our hearts, and just where these forces are directed determines how useful or harmful they are."

It all clicked. Over time, I realized this wasn't just about skiing—it was about life itself.

By early December, things at the Ramada weren't going well. The chaotic rhythm of "order, order, order" from Don's Butcher Block kept flashing back in my mind. The pace felt too frantic, too familiar, and I knew I needed a change.

I'd heard that LTV, the Texas-based corporation that owned Steamboat Ski Resort, was hiring for maintenance. Someone mentioned the supervisor's name—Paul—so the next morning, I made a bold decision. I skipped my shift at the Ramada and headed straight to the mountain, arriving at 6:00 a.m., determined to meet Paul.

I spotted him and his crew shoveling snow, so I walked right up and said, "I'm ready to work. How can I help?"

Paul looked up, startled but intrigued. "I'm busy right now," he said, "but come see me at 9:00 in my office."

A jolt of nerves shot through me—I had just gambled my job and my meals on this. There was no turning back.

At 8:50, I entered the hotel, made my way through the kitchen, and asked where the elevator to the maintenance shop was. Downstairs, I found Paul on the phone. He motioned for me to sit at the table outside his office while I waited. One of the crew offered me coffee, and I accepted, glancing through the window into Paul's office every now and then, trying to read the situation.

Finally, Paul waved me in.

"The job's simple—shoveling snow, hauling wood to the condo units. We work four ten-hour days, starting at 5:00 a.m. with an hour for lunch. Can you handle that?"

"I was here this morning ready to work, wasn't I?" I replied.

Paul gave me a curious look, half amused and half impressed. "Fill out these forms," he said, "and you've got a job for the winter."

I walked out of that hotel with a grin so big it hurt my cheeks. Most people came to Steamboat to ski, to live the life of a carefree ski bum. But not me. I came to live in the Rockies, to work hard, to breathe in the cold mountain air, and to be surrounded by the landscape I'd always dreamed of.

I didn't want an easy job like parking attendant or a cushy night shift. I wanted to be out there, in the thick of it, and I'd just landed the perfect job—complete with a season pass. How cool was that?

The Rhythm of Work

I worked four ten-hour days during the ski season, mainly shoveling snow and hauling firewood up to the condos. Snow shoveling turned out to be surprisingly meditative and visually rewarding—a task that suited my love for rhythm and repetition. There was something soothing about the motion—plunging the shovel into the snow, lifting it, and watching the landscape transform with each pass.

Often, when I arrived at a snow-covered walkway or set of stairs, the path was invisible, a blank canvas begging for order. But with that first plunge of the shovel, the walkway gradually emerged, and with it came immense satisfaction—from chaotic drifts to a neat, clear path framed by uniform snowbanks.

Our shovels, deep and wide like those used in horse stalls at camp, scooped large amounts of snow efficiently. Each scoop brought a small but tangible sense of control and completion—something I often craved. One scoop at a time, the world around me became more orderly, the rhythm perfectly attuned to my nature.

To avoid wearing myself out too quickly, I alternated arms—left, then right. This gave me balance and helped maintain a steady rhythm. Once I settled into the groove, I entered a meditative state.

The work flowed smoothly, and before long, the entire walkway was cleared. I'd pause, look up, and feel a deep sense of satisfaction. What had been an indistinct, snow-covered stretch minutes ago now lay clean and defined, down to the cement or wood beneath.

Being outdoors in the sun and fresh air revitalized me, making the labor almost effortless. And then there were the views. This was before the Sheraton took over the ski resort, before the towering condos blocked the sweeping scenery around the ski plaza. The entire Yampa Valley lay in view—the train winding in from Oak Creek and the distant flat-topped mountains stretching across the horizon.

If the day's work wasn't enough exercise, I'd head to the gym in the condo building afterward. After working out, I'd unwind in the sauna for fifteen or twenty minutes, letting the heat seep into my bones after hours in the cold. Then I'd multitask: start dinner, take a shower, check on the food, get dressed, and eat.

With work starting at 5:00 a.m., I had to be up by 4:00 to catch a ride down by the highway. This meant lights out by 8:00 p.m., leaving little time to socialize with my roommates, Jim and Lynn.

After dinner, I'd retreat to my room, open my notebook, and reflect on the day. I'd read over previous entries, adding new thoughts and observations.

That quiet time at the end of each day became my sanctuary—a space to unwind, reflect, and absorb the steady rhythm of my life. I loved it.

Meditation

Winter made it difficult to venture beyond the shoveled pathways, confining my physical world to the narrow trails carved through snow. Yet, through my journaling, I found a way to explore my mind.

Pot became my escape from the harshness of reality, offering temporary detours into a calmer, more introspective state. But when my supply ran out, I scribbled on the cover of my notebook: *Life is the*

Drug. It was a declaration, a reminder to myself that there was something deeper to tap into, something beyond artificial highs.

By this point, I was living on a whole different plane than when I'd left Cleveland. The city's noise and chaos felt like a distant memory. Here, surrounded by mountains and immersed in solitude, my perspective shifted.

Life felt raw, stripped down to its essentials, and every moment seemed more vivid and meaningful. It wasn't just the physical landscape that had changed—it was me. I was discovering new layers of myself, and with each passing day, I felt more attuned to the rhythms of the world around me.

My living situation was sparse. I had no real furniture except for a chair I pulled from a dumpster and some wood planks I'd turned into shelves. I tried making a rope bed but found the floor more comfortable.

Maybe it was the mummy bag I slept in—tightly wrapped, cocooned in warmth—that helped me sleep so well. At the time, I didn't know why, but now it reminds me of Temple Grandin's squeeze machine, designed to provide deep pressure for comfort and calm. I wouldn't discover I was on the autism spectrum until I was 45, but it makes sense now why that tight, secure feeling helped me sleep better than I ever had.

Most nights, I'd meditate as I drifted off. I'd read about a form of meditation that involved becoming aware of your body, starting with your toes and working your way up to your head. At first, it was hard to pull off, but within days, I became more attuned to each part of my body. I could feel my toes, feet, ankles, legs, fingers, arms, torso, and head in turn. Eventually, I was able to hold that meditative state long enough to drift into sleep.

After several nights of this, I began to expand the practice. I'd go through the same process—body part by body part—but then I'd extend my awareness to the room itself. I could sense the floor beneath me, the chair at my feet, the bookshelf to my left, the closet behind and to my right, the door at my head, and the light hanging from the ceiling.

I even became aware of the single window I left cracked open for fresh air. And then, something remarkable happened. My consciousness moved outside, through that opening in the window. I saw the view over Steamboat, the road leading up to the condo, and soon I was seeing everything from a few hundred feet above.

I kept expanding, floating over Rabbit Ears Pass, out to Kremmling, and beyond. I could see Steamboat's position in Colorado, its proximity to Denver, and the plains of Kansas stretching out from there. I even sensed the turmoil of the country—Jimmy Carter's challenges and how far removed it all felt from the peacefulness of Steamboat.

It was as if I could feel the pulse of the whole country from that vantage point. There was no sense of time, just peace. Slowly, I brought myself back, retracing my steps over Steamboat, through the window, and back into my body, lying on the floor of my room.

Today, I reflect on how experiences like that were once considered signs of mental instability. But I think perceptions have changed as the Western world has become more attuned to Eastern philosophy. What was really happening wasn't instability; I was tapping into the mental images I had gathered throughout my days.

I worked outside, walked all over town, and observed my surroundings with care. I'd seen the town's streetlights, the snowplows in the early morning, the night sky. During the day, I looked at the mountains while shoveling snow. I had maps from my drive to Steamboat, and I was always increasing my awareness.

As I quieted my mind and relaxed, those subconscious images I'd collected surfaced. My mind pieced them together, showing me Steamboat from my room, then from above, and finally the larger landscape. It wasn't an out-of-body experience—it was a heightened awareness. I saw how everything connected, and in that quiet space, it all made sense.

My time in Steamboat provided so many insights. I spent hours thinking and writing, sorting through everything I'd seen in life, trying to boil it down to some essence. One surprising realization was about sexual relationships—I saw how people were often seeking something simple and primal, though I struggled to articulate it without sounding crude.

I also noticed how I was influenced by the times. I wrote, *"You are you and I am I; don't try to change me, and I won't try to change you"*, thinking it was my own original thought. But fifteen years later, I learned that it was actually Fritz Perls' "Gestalt Prayer," which summed up the mindset of the 1960s:

"I do my thing and you do your thing. I am not in this world to live up to your expectations, And you are not in this world to live up to mine. You are you, and I am I, and if by chance we find each other, it's beautiful. If not, it can't be helped."

It's funny how, I had no idea so many others were feeling the same way. I must have absorbed these ideas subconsciously through music, TV, and movies. It makes me wonder what concepts and views today's youth are absorbing from their media.

My notebook held other thoughts about how to live life:

Believe yourself, Be in command, Know why you are
Live your dreams, Enjoy the present, Remember the past
Be wise, Act smart, Live comfortably
Go with the feeling. Don't try to explain it or you'll lose the experience.
Learn to love people as you do your music. Each has a different song to sing.

You don't make friends. You acquire them.

That winter, I also experienced the loss of my grandmother, my father's mother. The last time I saw Gram was on New Year's Eve. She had seemed peaceful, more so than the last time I'd visited her in Cleveland. Just a month later, she passed away from a heart attack. Her death hit me hard, and I found myself reflecting deeply on the fragility of life.

Later, I wrote in my notebook:

Death is hard to comprehend. A heart attack may kill the person, but it also attacks all the hearts that loved them. Here today, gone tomorrow. Grief is good, but it can kill you if it lasts too long. Use that energy you'd spend on grief to fortify your memories of the person and to love those still in your life.

Pushed by Passion

Skiing that year had been incredible. I'd never skied so hard or so well. With a free season pass and three-day weekends spent carving through Steamboat's famous champagne powder, *Inner Skiing* had transformed not only my technique but also my perspective on life. Each run felt like a meditation—fluid, rhythmic, and freeing. Yet, as the season wound down, I sensed an undercurrent of restlessness.

I had fulfilled a childhood dream by living in the Rockies, surrounded by the grandeur of snow-capped peaks and crisp mountain air. But as exhilarating as it had been, I began to feel the weight of its limitations. Photography, the one thing that truly ignited my passion, seemed to lack a clear path here. The mountains had given me clarity, but now they seemed to hem me in. I opened my notebook, hoping to unravel my thoughts.

March 25th:
Only two more months here. Life has been hard, challenging, nice, worthwhile, but changing. I've been thinking a lot about what I want to do, which must mean I don't care to stay here. Why have that on your mind if you're happy where you are?

This restlessness wasn't new—it echoed the undercurrent of my life. A few days later, I returned to my notebook, grappling with my identity and the many roles I'd played, as if trying to piece together a puzzle.

Tonight I was thinking . . . sometimes I feel that the things I do— photography, skiing, talking—are just parts I'm playing. I've been so many things: baby, camper, skier, garbage man, hippy, college student, stoner, cook, hitch-hiker, traveler, maintenance man. I've driven boats, cars, motorcycles, snow cats, horses. *A friend once said to me, "You are what you think others think you are." But who am I really?*

The question lingered, heavy and unresolved. My life had been a series of chapters, each one shaped by the roles I stepped into, but none of them felt like the full picture. Still, there was one truth I kept returning to: photography.

You have talent; you should always exercise it, I wrote. *Remember how you became good at riding horses? It took practice. Photography is the same. Don't push it; it will come.*

That realization brought a flicker of reassurance, but I still felt on the cusp of something greater—something undefined. I kept writing, hoping to capture a sense of direction:

In life, we do the things we like doing, and if we keep doing them, we get better. Skills take time. Look at how long it took you to learn to ride a bike or write your name. But if it's worth having, it's worth working for.

These reflections felt like breadcrumbs leading me forward, but the bigger questions persisted. Was I done? Had I reached my final destination in Steamboat, in the Rockies? Or was I holding onto something that had already given me all it could? Was Steamboat keeping me from something bigger—from my true potential?

By mid-June, the answer was clearer. *Almost eight months in Steamboat,* I wrote. *It was good to step out of life and look at it fully. I found out some of the things I want to do.* The mountains had been a sanctuary, a place to recalibrate and rediscover myself. But now, it was time to take what I'd learned and apply it elsewhere.

Steamboat had been a dream, a place where I'd grown and reflected. But dreams evolve. The town had served its purpose, providing a backdrop for self-discovery. Now, it was time to move forward, to find a place where my passion for photography could flourish. I had lived out one chapter of my life, but I was ready to start the next. Steamboat had been the stage for growth, but the world beyond the Rockies beckoned with new possibilities.

* * *

I sat there, on the couch, flipping through the notebook, the familiar spiral edges rough against my fingertips. Each page was a snapshot of my younger self—raw, idealistic, and full of questions. I couldn't help but smile at some of the scribbled thoughts, so earnest in their quest for understanding. What had happened to that version of me? Life, I supposed, with all its twists and detours. But maybe he wasn't entirely lost—maybe he was still in there, just waiting to be rediscovered.

The apartment around me was quiet, the last remnants of my recent move still scattered in half-unpacked boxes. I closed the notebook and set it on the coffee table, a physical link between my past and present. Steamboat had been a dream, a place where I'd learned to live with intention. Now, here I was, a world away from those snowy peaks, but the lessons from that time still resonated.

I glanced at the clock. Tomorrow would be another day of work, another step forward in this new chapter. My next trip to Cleveland loomed on the horizon, the house waiting to reveal its stories. But tonight, I let myself linger in the echoes of that twenty-year-old's thoughts, a quiet reminder that life is a series of evolving dreams.

With that, I turned out the light and headed to bed, ready to face whatever came next. Life never stops moving.

James S. Harper

In Pursuit of Photography

"Ladies and gentlemen, the captain has turned off the fasten seatbelt sign. You are free to get up and move about the cabin."

Once again, I was seven miles high, heading to Cleveland for the second time. I stood to retrieve my cassette tape recorder from the overhead compartment, but as I opened it, I paused. Looking down the aisle, I noticed most passengers were already plugged into their laptops. No movie on this flight—not long enough to bother, I guess. I had a lot on my mind, and maybe I should have been focusing on what needed to be done in Cleveland.

Sighing, I squeezed back into my seat and ordered two cocktails. I pulled a pen from my jacket and began jotting down a list of things to do: *Find burial plot, see funeral home, finish sorting...* I paused, staring at the paper. What a time in my life.

My older brother was relentless, hammering me with demands and threats about suing over Mom's will. She wasn't even dead yet, and he was already talking lawsuits. Meanwhile, my own divorce was a mess. My marriage had barely lasted three years before I lost trust in my wife.

Oddly enough, I could see now that she shared similar traits with my siblings. It made sense why I'd been attracted to her, she was just like my brothers and sister. But in this case, that wasn't a good thing.

And then there was work. The company that had acquired us was firing people left and right, without even understanding the importance of some of the folks they were letting go.

It felt like every part of my life was the same, just demands and complaints from all sides.

I knocked back the first drink quickly and opened a second vodka to finish off the tonic. My thoughts drifted to the last time Cleveland had truly felt like home. I was living with my older brother—the same one now threatening me—while in pursuit of photography as a career.

127

I remembered how my high school hadn't offered any real art or creative classes, like photography. That could have been a turning point, a chance to see if I had any talent or if photography was something I could actually make a living from. It might have given me the structure to make it pay for itself, but instead, I was left stumbling forward on my own—driven only by my aspiration to grow as a photographer.

Even then, I didn't seem to fit in. Everyone around me was content with the status quo, but I wanted more. I was in my mid-twenties and couldn't stop myself from reaching for the stars. MTV had just launched, and the possibilities in music videos and photography seemed endless. I wanted to be part of that world so badly.

It was a different time in my life, not as fulfilling as Steamboat, but it had its own edge. I felt alive, like there was a world of possibilities waiting for me, and I didn't care about conforming.

By the spring of 1984, I'd had enough of Cleveland. I needed to break free and be in a place where photography truly thrived. In the pages of photo magazines, it was all about color, Robert Farber's soft, dream-like images, Peter Turner's vibrant Cibachrome prints, and Joel Meyerowitz's scenes from Cape Cod. All saturated in color, all full of life.

I liked the B&W work of Edward Weston and Ansel Adams, and admired the creativity of Jerry Uelsmann's composites, but their gray tones mirrored the gloom of Cleveland itself. For seven years, I'd learned photography with black and white film because it was cheaper and easier than color. But now I wanted more.

I wanted to immerse myself in color, in life. My options were New York City, Chicago, or Los Angeles. I chose L.A. for its vibrant color photography and its warm climate. After all, I only had my motorcycle to make the trip, and I needed a warm place where I could thrive.

So, in October of that year, I left Cleveland behind. I set out for Los Angeles, determined to improve my photographic skills and dive headfirst into color photography. Thinking back now, it was the right choice. But sitting on this flight, heading back to Cleveland, I couldn't help but wonder what it all added up to.

I was almost 27, and the last six years had been some of the most miserable of my life—floundering, unsure of where to go or what to do, and stubbornly dismissing advice that didn't align with what I thought I wanted.

I had tried college, but when that became hopeless, I attempted to make it as a photographer. "Starving artist" was more accurate than I wanted to admit. I called myself a freelance photographer, but really, it felt like everyone just wanted me to work for free.

I apprenticed under several photographers, each with their own style, and heard the same thing from art directors: "You'd be bored taking the same photos day in and day out." Maybe they were right.

I had visions of living the glamorous life of an art photographer, but I had no idea what it truly took to succeed. The reality was, only a rare few who were truly, innovatively creative managed to make a living in photography. Most others were just good businessmen, selling photography as their product.

My experiences bouncing from ad agency to ad agency felt just as disheartening. Agencies wanted to see your most creative work, photos that could impress the elites of Fifth Avenue. But once they saw that you had creativity, they handed you assignments that were the complete opposite.

They'd ask you to photograph a plain glass of water on a gray background with straight lighting. That was it. They didn't want creativity, they wanted the predictable, the safe, the mundane. Sure, you had to show creative photos to get your foot in the door, but the actual work was as boring as it could get.

It was a harsh reality to accept, but these businesses weren't interested in unique or thoughtfully composed perspectives—they wanted a dependable product, a predictable image. Photography wasn't really about technique or vision; it came down to who you knew. The more I experienced this, the more I realized that success in photography wasn't just about creativity; it was about playing the game, about delivering precisely what was expected without pushing any boundaries.

Before I left for L.A., I had the opportunity to drive Grandpa to Florida, a trip he had made every year for as long as I could remember. Mabel, his third wife of fifteen years, had passed away from cancer earlier that year, and Grandpa needed someone to help with the drive. I had flown down in the spring to bring him back to Cleveland, and just before I set off for L.A. in the fall, I drove him south again and flew back.

That drive became unforgettable—a rare moment of one-on-one time with Grandpa before he passed away two years later. I saw a different side of him on that trip, a softer, more reflective man than the commanding lawyer I had heard about growing up.

He would light up during our evening cocktail stops, relishing the small ritual of catching the bartender's attention, a bit of charm and vanity lingering in the way he enjoyed fooling people about his age. But there was sadness too.

As we passed places he and Mabel had stopped before, I could see the weight of her absence in his eyes. Coming from a divorced family, it was strange for me to witness a marriage in my family that seemed built on real love and companionship. Their bond stood in stark contrast to the fractured relationships I had grown up with.

It wasn't until after Grandpa had recovered from his stroke that my mother shared something that struck me deeply. One day, he had told her that, in some way, he understood what it might be like to struggle with dyslexia. Hearing that from him meant more than I could put into words, because speaking—something so natural for most people—had never felt effortless for me.

I often stumbled over my words, pausing mid-sentence as I grasped for the right one, only to have my thoughts outrun my ability to say them. My mind rarely worked in a straight line; instead, it darted ahead, stacking ideas before I could finish the first.

These tangents weren't random to me—they were connected, but to others, they must have seemed like I couldn't finish a simple thought. My ADHD only amplified this, pushing multiple ideas to the front at once. To someone listening, it might have sounded like I was lost, but in reality, I was juggling too many threads, struggling to pull just one into focus.

Grandpa, though, understood. A corporate lawyer by trade, words had once been his weapon of choice, his mastery. But after his stroke, even with Mabel's help, some words slipped away from him.

I saw the frustration in his eyes when the right one wouldn't come, the silent battle behind them. Sometimes he'd get it, sometimes he wouldn't. And when he didn't, he'd throw his arms up in a half-defeated, half-joking way and mutter, *"Phooey."*

When my mother told me he could relate to my dyslexia, I found it hard to believe. No one had ever acknowledged the way I struggled to get words out—at least not in a way that suggested understanding. Yet, in his own way, he had. He didn't just see it; he felt it. It wasn't exactly the same, but it was close enough for him to offer something I hadn't often felt in life: empathy.

That drive to Florida wasn't just about getting him from one place to another. It gave me something more—a connection I hadn't expected, a moment of recognition I hadn't realized I needed. He would be gone two years later, but I would carry that conversation with me for the rest of my life.

Looking back, I wish I had learned earlier to appreciate time with the older generations. When we're young, we focus so much on how different we are from our parents and grandparents, convinced we'll never become like them.

But as time passes, we start to see the pieces of them in ourselves—their gestures, their stubbornness, their quiet battles. We realize, sometimes too late, how much there was to learn from them if we had only taken the time to listen.

On our way to Florida, we stopped by a Greg Alexander's studio in Nashville. Earlier that spring, I had received a flyer for one of his workshops. The image on it caught my eye—it was far more creative than anything I had seen in Cleveland. So, I packed up my motorcycle and rode down for the weekend.

Seeing Greg's studio in person was inspiring. Sure, he had the typical pouty model posing for photos, but what really struck me was the creative energy in his work. Greg was an exceptionally imaginative photographer.

We parked the car in an alley beside his loft-style studio. Grandpa and I walked in, and I'm pretty sure Greg thought we were just a couple of bums who wandered in off the streets of Nashville. I mentioned I had attended his workshop and that I was heading to L.A.. Greg brought up the Black Book offices in Hollywood.

For the past two years, I had been thumbing through *Black Book* for photo inspiration, admiring the level of creativity in it. Hearing Greg mention it felt like a sign that I was on the right path, kind of like in *Journey to the Center of the Earth,* when they would find the "A S" marker at the end of each episode, letting them know they were headed in the right direction.

I had a similar experience when I left for Steamboat Springs. There's something so comforting about these signs, those moments of clarity when you feel assured that you're on the right track. Usually, though, it's only in hindsight that you recognize them. If we put too much weight into what we "think" are signs in the moment, we risk misinterpreting them and giving ourselves false hope.

After dropping Grandpa off in Florida, I flew back to Cleveland, my mind already set on heading to L.A.. I had been considering it since late spring. This wasn't a quick decision like my seven-week prep for Steamboat; this time, I gave myself six months of mental preparation. I would leave in October, right when our apartment lease was up.

I planned to make the cross-country trip on my motorcycle, a 1983 Honda 650 Nighthawk. It wasn't the biggest bike for such a journey, but it was all I had. My old station wagon, which had carried my photo gear on countless shoots, just wasn't reliable enough. Besides, I had always dreamed of riding a motorcycle across the U.S. This was my chance to make that dream happen.

I had outfitted my bike with a bag strapped to the gas tank, which was perfect for holding maps, rain gear, and my Nikon equipment, making it easy to grab my camera whenever I spotted a shot. The bike also had large saddlebags, creating a flat surface across the back half of the seat. That flat spot was ideal for strapping on my tent and tripod.

Ansel Adams had his station wagon with a camera platform, but I had my nimble motorcycle as my trusty steed.

To keep everything dry, I used plastic garbage bags as a waterproof lining. The setup didn't hold much, but at that point, all I owned were my Nikons, some clothes, and my mummy sleeping bag. My Hasselblads, enlargers, and other darkroom gear were stored in Dad's basement.

It was early morning when I pushed the bike out of the apartment garage. The day was cool and overcast, a typical autumn morning in Cleveland. As I double-checked the straps in a final inspection, a wave of solitude washed over me.

I had said my goodbyes to my family the night before. My older brother had already left for work, and now, the unknown stretched out before me. The moment mirrored my departure for the Rockies six years earlier—charged with adrenaline and nerves. Nothing tethered me, as if I were leaping off the high dive into uncharted waters. It was just me and my bike at the bottom of the ramp, ready to go.

The wind rustled the leaves, creating that familiar, gentle hush that only autumn can bring. I wrapped my scarf snugly around my neck, zipped up my jacket, and slid on my helmet. Taking a final look around, I swung my leg over the bike and fired it up.

The engine's hum was muffled through the helmet but reverberated off the garage walls. I let it idle for a moment, giving the throttle a couple of quick twists to feel its power. Then, with a decisive click, I shifted into first gear and headed up the ramp, out onto the street, and toward the highway.

My first destination was The Home Ranch, a dude ranch outside Steamboat Springs where my sister was living after working there that summer. I planned to head south on I-71 to I-70, thinking the southern route would be warmer than taking I-80.

But less than an hour into the trip, I was freezing. The weather turned wet and colder than I expected. I was only wearing jeans, and the wind cut through them like a knife.

When I pulled off at the Ashland exit, memories of my time there came flooding back. I hadn't been to Ashland College in years, but suddenly I was remembering walking across campus on crisp mornings, the quiet streets, the small-town feel that had offered some sense of shelter, even though I'd never fully fit in. It was a place where

I had tried, for a brief time, to find direction, but the feeling of being adrift had always remained.

Lost in thought, I rummaged through my tank bag, looking for something warmer for my hands. When I didn't find anything, I stopped at a store and picked up a pair of glove liners. Back at my bike, I pulled out the old rain suit I'd kept from my days at Brandywine. I added an extra pair of socks and the ski pants I'd packed at the last minute. Even though it wasn't raining, I hoped the layers would keep the wind from cutting through my clothes.

Back on I-71, I began flexing my fingers and toes, trying to get the blood circulating again. By the time I reached Columbus, the clouds had broken, and the sun came out. It's amazing how a little sunlight can change everything.

The day turned into a perfect autumn day, with crisp air and golden light that seemed to brighten not just the scenery but my mood. With the sun shining, the ride became a whole lot more enjoyable, even though it was still cool. That bit of warmth from the sun made all the difference.

The motorcycle ride down to Nashville was the perfect preparation for my longer journey. On that trip, I got to know my bike inside and out, how it handled, how far I could push it, and exactly how long I could go on a tank of gas before switching to the reserve. It turned out to be about 140–150 miles per tank, including the reserve. There wasn't a fuel gauge, so I reset the tripmeter every time I filled up.

I also figured out that I could lay my chest down on the tank bag, which not only gave me an alternative sitting position but also cut down on wind resistance. I didn't have a windshield, nor did I want one. Feeling the wind in my face was part of the experience, part of what made riding a motorcycle so exhilarating.

I rode all day, with no agenda other than the road in front of me. I'd refuel every couple of hours, which gave me a chance to stretch my legs and check over the bike. It was just me and the machine, no spare tire, and definitely no nodding off.

By late afternoon, I was crossing Kansas, watching dark clouds gather ever since the state line. Soon enough, I found myself caught in a full-blown rainstorm. My rain suit helped, but it funneled all the water from my chest downward, soaking my pants in no time.

Cars were pulling over to the shoulder, but I kept going. Then I spotted another biker taking shelter under an overpass and decided to join him. I pulled off my helmet just in time to hear him say, "Did you see the tornado?" as he pointed to the south.

"Nope, where is it?"

"Well, I saw it about a mile back, then I spotted this overpass and pulled off."

"Wow, it's been raining forever," I said.

"Yep, but looks like we're at the tail end of it."

With that, he buttoned up his rain suit, got on his bike, and took off. I hung back for a few minutes, watching the rain taper off, before heading out. The skies cleared, leaving a few scattered clouds behind.

Several hours later, after cutting across Kansas, the sun began to set—a spectacular sight. A bright orange ball of fire dipped beneath the clouds before vanishing below the horizon.

But that was hours ago. Now, it was dark, and I was grateful for my strong headlight. Then, out of nowhere, one of the scariest moments of my life happened—I nodded off.

"Shit."

My palms went sweaty, my heart raced, and I was instantly wide awake. But I couldn't trust it would last. Spotting a small hotel at the next exit, I pulled off. Fleas or no fleas, I was done for the day.

The next morning was cold, but the sunrise promised clear skies. I set off with Steamboat Springs in my sights, hoping to make it there by nightfall. This time, I watched in awe as the Rocky Mountains slowly rose from the horizon. Early in the afternoon, I passed through Denver, and before long, I was riding over Berthoud Pass. The pace quickened, my excitement building as I neared the mountains. It felt like coming home.

I met up with my sister just before sunset. We drove into Steamboat for dinner, where she filled me in on how wonderful her summer had been. Being her brother, I was genuinely happy for her. After a few beers and some burritos, I was more than ready to turn in for the night.

The next day, she showed me around the ranch, and we did a little hiking and sightseeing. The place was quiet, in the low season, or what some people call mud season, though spring is definitely muddier. A day of rest, free from the wind, was just what I needed. But the next day, it was time to hit the road again.

I left early that morning, heading down Route 131 to I-70. By the time I reached Grand Junction, my mileage showed 72 miles on the tank, and I figured I had a good 70 miles left before I needed to refuel. But as I crossed the Colorado-Utah border, I realized I'd miscalculated.

"Damn."

The highway stretched out into nothing but desolate land, and it hit me: I was going to run out of gas. I couldn't believe it. Usually, it was safe to assume there'd be a gas station within 70 miles, but this was the West—vast, empty, and unforgiving. I hadn't seen any signs warning me, but my mind flashed images of those old signs saying, "No gas for the next 100 miles."

I let up on the throttle, trying to think through my predicament. Turning back wasn't an option—it was at least 30 miles back to Grand Junction, and I had maybe 30, 35 miles left in the tank. Either way, I was going to run out of gas, so I might as well push forward.

Then, out of nowhere, I pictured a pickup truck with a red gas can in the back, the kind you see in movies. I didn't have time to dwell on it. I knew it wasn't behind me, so I had to get a move on and find that truck. I throttled back up to 70 MPH, straining my eyes to spot this imaginary savior.

Soon, I saw a truck, but no gas can. I kept going. The tripmeter read 125 miles, still no sign of a station. The road became a little hilly, with a few long curves that limited my line of sight.

130 miles. Still nothing.

At 135 miles, I spotted a black speck in the distance, but something on its left side looked strange.

"Shit!"

The main tank went dry. I quickly turned the petcock to release the reserve gas.

"Damn, I'm getting worse mileage on this tank."

As I got closer, I saw that the black speck was a truck, and that odd thing on the left side? No way… could it be? Was it red? I sped up to 75 MPH, closing in fast. Sure enough, it was a red gas can! But was it filled with gas? Who cares! I had to catch them.

I passed the truck and glanced over to see who was driving—an older man and his wife. I accelerated ahead, far enough to pull over and flag them down. Just as I expected, the engine sputtered and died. I jumped off the bike and started waving my arms, praying they would stop.

They did.

The small pickup rolled to a stop a few feet behind me. The driver's door opened as I walked over.

"Out of gas?" he asked.

"Yep. I miscalculated—should have gassed up in Grand Junction," I replied.

"We have some. Let me get it."

A wave of relief washed over me. "Can you spare a gallon or so? I think that's all I'll need to reach the next gas station."

"We'll just fill you up—no need to take any more chances." He instinctively walked over to grab the can of gas.

I watched as he filled my tank. When I reached into my pocket to offer payment, he interrupted, "No, no need. I'm glad to help."

And that was it. He returned to his truck, and I sat back on my bike, ready to head off.

Wow—he wouldn't take a dime for it, either, I thought. I thanked him, and I thanked Him.

I made it out of Utah with a valuable lesson learned: in the West, view your tank as half-empty, not half-full. From then on, I filled up every time I saw a gas station.

The weather had shifted from the cold plains to the dry heat of the Nevada desert. I was making good time on I-15, but soon I noticed my bike wobbling. Something wasn't right. Fear crept in as I realized I might lose control, so I pulled over. Sure enough, the back tire was low on air.

"Damn it."

There was nothing out there but hot desert, and I had no spare. I put the bike up on its center stand and examined the tire. Eventually, I found the culprit—a screw lodged deep into the rubber. Thankfully, the tire was tubeless, but I wasn't sure what to do next.

I thought about pulling the screw out but then remembered something one of the Masters at Olin had told us: he had found a screw in his car tire and had screwed it "in" tighter, sealing the leak. It was worth a shot. I twisted the screw in tighter, then used the can of Fix-a-Flat I had packed, inflating the tire.

At first, I doubted my makeshift repair, but after a few miles, I started to feel more confident it would hold. By the time I reached Las Vegas, I found a bike shop to make a proper repair.

The tire repair cost me about an hour, but I was grateful to have gotten there before the shop closed for the day. Afterward, I hit the road again, with Santa Monica as my final destination, just four hours away.

It was dark by the time I descended from San Bernardino into the sprawling lights of the L.A. basin. I was amazed by the sheer amount of traffic and how the lights stretched endlessly in every direction. I spotted signs for the Santa Monica Freeway and thought I was getting close, but forty-five minutes later, I was still on the 10 Freeway.

"How big is this place?"

The miles of highways all blurred together, and I had no real idea where I was headed, other than Santa Monica, a name that sounded familiar. Before I knew it, the 10 had turned into the 1, and I found myself riding past the beach. Somehow, I managed to get off the highway and onto the regular city streets of Santa Monica.

The day's ride had taken its toll. After more than sixteen hours on the road, combined with three previous days of battling relentless winds, I was utterly exhausted. I spotted some motels on Wilshire Boulevard. The streets seemed clean, but the motels didn't. Still, I wasn't in any position to be picky. I checked in, unloaded what I could, and locked up the bike, praying it would still be there in the morning. I half-slept through the night, keeping one ear open for any alarming sounds.

Morning came, but the noise of the road still buzzed in my head. I took stock of my situation: no credit cards, just cash—about $400 and change. I didn't know a soul in L.A., nor did I have a plan other than *go to L.A.*

After riding through an hour of solid city last night, I felt lost, overwhelmed, and exhausted. *"What have I done?"* It was a far cry from my adventurous days heading off to Steamboat Springs, where the excitement of the unknown was still met with a laid-back energy. Steamboat had its own thrill, but it was a small, welcoming place that made you feel like you belonged, even if you were just passing through. L.A., on the other hand, was running at full speed, and I quickly realized you couldn't slip here—not when you were just one in a sea of millions. Now, I just felt worn out.

I loaded up the bike and found a McDonald's. Sitting there with a cup of coffee, I stared at my bike, wondering what to do next. Part of me wanted to leave. I had just arrived, and already I was thinking about heading back. But how could I? Cleveland had been a nightmare—art judges telling me not to bother entering shows, fragile egos everywhere. It was all about who you knew, and as someone introverted and, on the spectrum, socializing had always been difficult.

How could I return, feeling defeated? No—I had to at least try.

As I sat there, my gaze drifted past my bike to a newspaper dispenser across the street. Maybe I should check the ads.

I walked over, grabbed the morning paper, and there it was: *Wanted: black & white printer, will train color.* Train for color! That was exactly what I wanted to learn.

Excited, I called immediately, but the guy was too busy to talk. After a few tries, still no luck. Determined not to miss this chance, I got directions to the lab and headed there in person.

Before going to the lab, I stopped at a newsstand. A photographer I had worked for used Agfa paper, and one of his black-and-white images had even appeared in a national Agfa ad. Flipping through a magazine, I found the ad and grabbed a copy—figuring it might help.

The two-story Deco façade loomed ahead, its clean geometric lines a relic of old Hollywood. I parked my bike in the alley with the others and walked in unannounced. Someone led me downstairs to the basement, where movie posters covered the walls—some familiar, others not. In the back, under two massive banks of lights, a guy was color-correcting prints. This had to be Dave.

"Dave, this guy saw your ad," someone called out, gesturing toward me.

Dave barely looked up. "Yeah, hi. I've got a lot to do," he muttered, disappearing into one of the darkrooms.

I stood there, taking in the rows of color separations—magenta, yellow, cyan, and black—laid out for precise printing. After a moment, Dave reappeared with a photo paper box in hand.

"I'll be right back. Need to run this through the processor," he said, vanishing again.

When he returned, he glanced at my helmet. "What kind of bike you got?"

"A Honda Nighthawk."

"Cool. I've got a V65 Magna. You park with the others? It's safe—they lock the gates at sunset."

"Yeah, that's where I parked. So… you need someone for black-and-white printing?"

I was nervous, the highway noise still buzzing in my head, but I pushed through. I held up the Agfa ad.

"I worked for the photographer who shot this."

Dave nodded, interested but cautious. "We're specialized here. Ad agencies send us layouts, and we have to match them exactly."

Sensing an opening, I blurted, "Give me a negative, and I'll show you what I can do." Somewhere in the process, my nerves faded. I almost surprised myself with the confidence in my voice.

Dave paused, then gave a small grin. "Okay. Follow me."

He led me to a darkroom. "Ever use a 4x5 Omega?"

"Yeah, I've got one back home."

"Good. Here's the chrome and the layout. Size it up and let me know when you're done."

It didn't take long. "Got it," I called out.

Dave checked my work. "Close, but here's the thing—you've gotta be exact, down to the pencil line." He adjusted the enlarger, aligning the layout perfectly. "There's paper in this box. Expose it for 45 seconds, then I'll show you the processor."

I followed his instructions, hoping every step would bring me closer to landing the job.

I ended up staying at the lab until 8, working on the images Dave gave me. We discussed how to dodge and burn to refine each print, and we seemed to hit it off. Dave, originally from West Virginia, had traveled Europe and, as I later learned, had connections to some major players in the art photography world.

As the evening wore on, he asked where I was staying. When I mentioned the dingy motel from the night before, he invited me to crash at his place in Sherman Oaks after we picked up some Thai food.

When we arrived, his wife, her music manager, and their roommates were having a full-on pajama party. A massive white rabbit with pink eyes—easily the size of a small dog—hopped between them like it was just another guest.

Welcome to California, I thought.

The next day, I met Paul, the owner, and it seemed I had been hired. I liked to think my printing skills landed me the job, but I later learned that Dave's wife was from Cleveland, which might have helped sway Paul's decision. Either way, I was now working at a major graphics lab in Hollywood, specializing in dye transfer and Cibachrome prints for the movie and record industries. It felt like we worked on at least 75% of the composites for movie posters, video boxes, and album covers.

Strangely enough, about a month later, while exploring the building, I found the offices of *Black Book*—the same publication Greg Alexander had mentioned. It felt like stumbling upon another carved signature of "A S," a confirmation that I was following a hidden path, step by step.

For the next four years, I built photo composites—what we called *strips*— for the movie and record studios. This was before Photoshop existed, so everything was done by hand, layer by painstaking layer. I worked with raw transparencies shot by some of Hollywood's top photographers, meticulously assembling images into seamless visuals. A *strip* was essentially an image built from multiple elements to create something entirely new.

I had always admired Jerry Uelsmann's black-and-white composites and had even entered my first major contest with a composite image. But now, I was doing it professionally, in color, for the movie industry. Seeing my work displayed on billboards and video boxes was surreal. It gave me something tangible to show for my efforts, and I felt a quiet pride whenever I could point to a poster and say, *I worked on that.*

Paul once explained how, back in New York, they used a technique called *emulsion stripping*—a delicate process where parts of a transparency's emulsion were physically removed and placed onto another piece of film to create a composite image. By the mid-1980s, we had moved to using Kodalith film, a high-contrast black-and-white film that developed into either pure black or completely clear areas. We used these *Kodalith masks* to block certain sections of photo paper from being exposed, allowing us to build complex images in layers.

Before photography, illustrators had been responsible for creating these types of images for advertising—Norman Rockwell being one of the most famous. But photography opened up endless possibilities. If an art director wanted an arm repositioned or needed an image that couldn't be captured in a single shot, we could build it through composite techniques. Movie posters became a perfect blend of illustration and photography, and composites allowed us to create the impossible.

I remember working on the poster for *Roxanne*, starring Steve Martin. He wasn't available for the promotional shoot, so we stripped his head onto another person's body—an everyday trick in our world.

There were two things that made working at the graphics lab such a perfect fit for me: the photography itself and the intricate process of creating a *strip*. New orders were placed in a box on the wall, and I was always eyeing it, eager to stay busy.

Most strips had three to five elements, each built from slides— what we called *chromes*—never negatives, since we were a Cibachrome lab. The chromes, usually 35mm but sometimes larger formats, each required a contrast control mask—a negative copy that balanced exposure.

Each chrome and mask had to be precisely aligned on a punched 4x5 support film, then sandwiched between glass to prevent any movement. Long exposures generated heat, sometimes causing the film to shift out of focus. The glass kept everything in place, but it also meant every surface—two per chrome, two per mask, and two per glass—had to be inspected under an 8x loupe for dust or imperfections. That added up to eight surfaces per image, multiplied by the three or four elements in each strip.

The process played right into how my brain worked. My ADHD spectrum mind was constantly engaged, tracking multiple variables and optimizing the workflow. I'd mount and mask all the chromes, lay out the composition, make test strips for color and exposure, then run them through the processor.

While the prints developed—a 20-minute process—I'd move on to the next element, keeping everything in motion. Once I had final test prints, I'd fine-tune exposure and color to seamlessly blend the elements. It was intricate, detail-driven work that demanded both precision and efficiency, and I thrived in it.

One of my more notable "happy accidents" happened in 1987 while working on the *Beverly Hills Cop II* movie poster. The composite featured Eddie Murphy leaning against the Beverly Hills sign, with a vivid sunset and palm trees in the background. The composite was made up of four separate images—Eddie Murphy, the Beverly Hills sign, the palm trees, and the sunset sky were all different layers.

The lab usually delivered the ad agency three prints, each with slight color variations. It had been a long day—starting before 8:00 AM—and I was pushing well past twelve hours. I was working on the last two versions simultaneously. I register-punched two pieces of photo paper, inserted them into the light-tight box, and carried them from room to room, exposing them on various easels to build the composite.

Cibachrome exposures were notoriously long compared to black-and-white prints. While B&W exposures might take ten to fifteen seconds, Cibachrome typically required sixty to ninety seconds, sometimes even longer. You'd sit in the dark, waiting—unless some dodging or burning was needed.

That night, I was exhausted. The last component to expose was the trees. I took out one sheet of photo paper, exposed the trees, put the paper back in the box. I rechecked everything before exposing the second sheet, but when I reached in the box . . . I froze. *Did I just expose the top sheet or the bottom one?* I couldn't remember.

Losing track mid-process was a nightmare with composites because each complete print could take fifteen minutes or more, and you wouldn't know if you'd made a mistake until after the 20-minute developing process. I thought, *I'm not going to jeopardize both sheets and have to start all over again. I'll just finish the process and hope for the best.*

When the prints finally came out, my fears were justified. I had missed exposing the palm tree background, and with Cibachrome, anything that doesn't get exposed turns black. So instead of the natural colors of the trees, the area came out solid black.

But as I looked at the print, I realized that this mistake actually looked better. The black silhouettes of the palm trees against the sunset gave the image more punch and contrast.

I wasn't in any position to tell the art director what to do, so I showed Paul and let him take it to the advertising agency. To my surprise, they loved the mistake. They came back and said, *"Do two more prints with the black trees."* So, in the end, it was my mistake that led to those black trees on the *Beverly Hills Cop II* poster.

Things like that make you feel like your work matters, like you really contributed to the final product. It gave me a little extra bounce in my step as I walked into the lab, knowing I had left my mark.

It was an incredible time, building these composites by hand. Every day, I worked with some of the most iconic images in the industry, pushing the limits of what we could create without the aid of computers. Those four years at the lab sharpened my photographic eye, and I realized this was exactly what I had been searching for when I left Cleveland in pursuit of a photo mecca.

* * *

The jolt of the plane hitting the runway and the roar of the reverse thrust snapped me out of my daze. Cleveland already? Those vodka tonics had knocked me out for the entire flight. The thoughts of Hollywood quickly faded as the reality of the tasks awaiting me the next day sank in. I grabbed my bag from the overhead compartment and headed off to pick up my rental car.

Where I Left Myself

Walking Among the Past

Arriving at Mom's house, I found it no warmer than before. My previous efforts were visible in the four piles of belongings taking shape in the living room, one for each child—including me.

My sister's pile was the largest, as she was the natural heir to the items passed down through the women in our family. Dishes, furniture, and keepsakes—all treasures from our mother's side—had been passed from mother to daughter, now finding their way to my sister. I was glad Mom had made a list of what she wanted each of us to have. In hindsight, if we siblings had gotten along better, perhaps a more equitable division could have been made. But these were Mom's wishes, not mine.

I stared at the piles one last time, then set the thermostat to 72 degrees and headed upstairs to bed.

The next morning, I got up early to visit our family's cemetery before my appointment at the funeral home. I hadn't been there since Grandpa's funeral about twenty years ago and wanted to refresh my memory of Mom's family burial plot. It took a little time driving around to find it.

The cemetery was meticulously cared for, its orderly rows of headstones quietly marking the passage of time. Finally, I found our tree-covered lot. The cemetery dated back to the mid-1860s, and my mother's family purchased the lot not long after it was established. I always found the lot striking, with its central granite monument carved with the original family name. Around it were 24 plots arranged neatly along the four sides.

I walked around, glancing at each headstone. Some names I vaguely recognized, while others had once been familiar. I was struck by the realization that these headstones represented over a hundred years of my mother's family's presence here. Yet, even as I thought this, I noticed how I automatically made the distinction between whose side of the family I was referring to. Perhaps that habit is a product of growing up in a divorced family, where everything was separated into sides rather than being part of one unified whole.

Mom's roots in Cleveland stretched back much further than Dad's, making her a sixth-generation Clevelander—over 150 years of family history. The earliest date of death was 1883, and the most recent was my grandmother's—Mom's mother, Granny, who passed away in the early 1980s.

Mom was born in the early 1930s into an affluent family. She followed in her mother's footsteps by attending the same private girls' school. In high school, she wrote for the school newspaper and became her father's co-pilot on cross-country flights before going on to work at a local publishing company.

Yet her privileged life wasn't without burdens. At just six years old, her parents divorced—a rarity at the time. What made it even more scandalous was that her parents, close friends with a Canadian couple, had swapped partners within a year.

The event made headlines in local newspapers across neighboring states. I remember her sharing this story with us as children, describing how unsettling it was to have reporters outside her home. I found it hard to believe, but while cleaning out her house, I found the articles she had saved, confirming the story.

I once saw an elementary school class photo of Mom when I was about ten. Her face looked so sad, and for the first time, I realized how far back her struggles must have gone—long before she became the woman I knew, devoted to her children yet carrying the weight of her past.

She was not yet seven when her parents divorced, and I can only imagine the arguments and confusion she endured. For a child, the turmoil of a divorce—especially in the late 1930s, when it was so rare— must have been deeply unsettling, made worse by reporters eager to uncover the scandal. Her earliest memories of marriage were steeped in conflict and separation, shaping how she later approached relationships and family life.

Coming from divorced parents, it was striking to see that almost all the headstones in the family plot belonged to husband-and-wife pairs—united even in death. Granny rested beside her second husband, the man she had stayed with until the end. But my mother's future resting place was different. She would lay alone, just on the other side of her mother's grave.

Staring at the empty space, the truth settled in—not just about where she would be laid to rest, but about how she had lived. She had been alone for much of her life. Even during her marriage, she always seemed somewhat separate, as though she existed alongside people rather than with them.

The divorce, meant to give her freedom, may have only deepened that isolation. Financial limitations forced her out of the suburb where she had grown up, severing ties with the friends of her youth. In the end, the only people truly in her life were her children—but even we grew up and moved on, leaving her more alone than ever.

I had seen it before, this loneliness, but only now did I understand how much of it I carried myself.

My father once told me, when I was still a teenager, that I reminded him of my mother in that way—alone, but seemingly unfazed by it. At that time in my life, I didn't think much of it. When you're living a certain way, it doesn't feel odd. A drunkard doesn't necessarily see himself as an alcoholic.

I had been sent to boarding school for my dyslexia, separated from the kids I'd grown up with, missing out on the typical high school experiences—the dances, the awkward trial and error of teenage relationships. Later, in college, I was four years behind my peers in dating, stumbling through encounters that felt scripted by some invisible handbook I never received.

It wasn't just circumstance. It was a pattern.

I was reminded of a moment from years earlier—visiting a high school friend and watching as his mother pulled him into a warm, effortless hug. The kind only a mother can give. A simple gesture, but one that struck me deeply.

I don't recall ever receiving a hug like that. My mother wasn't unkind or indifferent, but there had always been a distance between us. Had she felt it too? Or was it simply the only way she knew how to be?

And now, standing in the quiet of the cemetery, I had to ask: Was this solitude woven into my genes, or was it something I had learned? Had my mother ever wanted more? Or had she, like me, grown tired of chasing connections that never felt quite right? Maybe solitude was easier. Maybe it was just what we knew.

I looked down at the space reserved for her—isolated, yet still tied by blood to the family plot—and wondered if I'd end up in a similar place. Alone, marked only by my name, watching from the outside even in death.

I glanced at the headstone of Granny's second husband and thought about how different her life had been from Mom's. Two husbands, two distinct chapters. Meanwhile, Mom had one marriage that dissolved, leaving her to raise four children alone. No new chapters, just an empty space beside her, a gap where another name should have been. Did she ever look at her parents' graves and wonder what went wrong for her?

It struck me then that we never talked about any of this. The regrets, the disappointments. Everything was just... quietly ignored. And now, with her dementia erasing the past, my chance for meaningful conversations was slipping away.

Even if I tried now, I'd be speaking to a version of her that no longer held those memories. I felt a pang of guilt, knowing I should have asked more questions when I could. But it's hard to see those things when you're young—especially when you're caught up in your own struggle to find your place in the world.

I took some pictures and then remembered that Grandpa's family burial plot was here too, in a different section. I drove over, appreciating the beauty and uniqueness of cemeteries.

Sleepy Hollow came to mind—the narrow, winding paths barely wide enough for a horse and cart, overgrown with ancient trees whose branches draped over graves, casting long, haunting shadows. This cemetery, however, couldn't have been more different. Although it was still very much winter, I could imagine the well-manicured lawns bathed in sunlight. The monuments, standing tall, were a testament to over a century of history. Midwinter had settled in, with bare trees silhouetted against a cold, gray sky, and the ground still frozen, showing no sign of green.

I parked and walked up the hill to their row of headstones. This section was more open, with few family monuments and even fewer trees. I went down the line—there was great-grandmother, Mabel, Grandpa, and Grandpa's father. I paused, looking at the death dates etched into the stones and realized that Grandpa's father had died when he was just four years old. Grandpa grew up fatherless for most of his life, and I got lost in that thought for a while.

My mother was raised by a man who had never had a father figure of his own. Dad once mentioned how his own father was constantly away on business trips. My mother grew up without reliable parental figures—her parents were wrapped up in their own lives after the divorce, leaving little room for active parenting.

While my father had a strong German mother who provided some stability, both of them lacked a consistent, daily father figure in their upbringing. It explained so much about my family—why my parents never seemed to have a close partnership and why emotional distance seemed woven into the family line.

My mother was raised by a man who never learned how to father, and my father, with his own father always away, had little guidance on how to be present. I wondered: how much did their lack of foundation shape my own choices?

My Old Haunt

As I reflected on the patterns that had shaped my life, my thoughts drifted to my own struggles for independence. My old apartment, the one I'd left behind when I moved to L.A., was nearby—just a block from the camera store where I had worked. On a whim, I decided to visit the neighborhood and stop by the local coffee shop to warm up.

Sitting there, memories from my second year living in that apartment surfaced — specifically, the year I'd finally had enough of working at the camera store. I didn't want to be a sales clerk; I wanted to be a photographer. The question loomed large in my mind: was I going to make a living at photography or not?

So, I quit. That year was a struggle. Money was tight, and I was never sure if I'd have enough to cover rent. Most nights, dinner was liver and onions — chicken liver cost only fifty cents. I'd eat it more times than I care to remember. Yet somehow, when the end of the month arrived and my expenses loomed, freelance work would come through just in time — never more, never less.

After finishing my coffee, I took a slow walk back to my car, passing by the old apartment. I circled the building since I couldn't go inside. The place looked just as it always had, with its 1930s architecture and faded brick walls. I wandered around to the side and down the ramp to the garage door.

My last memory here was doing a final check of my motorcycle before setting off for L.A.. The garage door, the walls, the driveway — all looked exactly the same, even though more than twenty years had passed.

I remembered the confidence I had in the unknown then — a far cry from how I felt now. I was so certain that leaving was the only way to put my life in Cleveland behind me for good. It was disheartening in some ways, but freeing in others. Why stay when you aren't understood and your aspirations don't fit those who make the rules?

It's strange how a single place can hold so much of your past, reminding you not just of what you did but also of what you didn't do. Standing there brought back all the 'what ifs,' the 'could'ves,' and the 'would'ves' that have silently lingered in my mind over the years. Those lingering thoughts that circle back to the decisions I made and the opportunities I passed up. It's easy to wonder how things might have turned out differently had I taken a different path.

There were moments when the doors of opportunity opened, but I hesitated to walk through them. For instance, someone once fed me a lead to shoot at a retail store, but that venture ended in failure. I had several dinners with a writer-producer who had created a 1960s TV series that I admired, but for some reason, I never talked to him about our shared interests during our time together. I'd heard too many stories about the wild parties in the Hollywood Hills, and I didn't want to get caught up in something I would regret the next day.

Early on, I understood that most photographers needed to be their own boss. They had to be businessmen as much as artists. I painfully learned this lesson as far back as my paper route—getting paid was never my strong suit. Most of the freelance jobs I took on barely covered my expenses, and in some cases, I walked away with nothing. It became evident that I didn't have the necessary skills to navigate the business side of photography.

That lack of business savvy made it even harder to figure out where I fit in the photography world. I wasn't willing to be a commercial photographer, executing someone else's vision, nor did I want to be a portrait and wedding photographer, where success depended more on running a business than on creativity.

Art photography, on the other hand, spoke to me—it was about capturing the unexpected, being moved by what I happened to see. But success in art photography required more than just an artist's eye. It demanded skills I struggled with: networking and marketing.

One such challenge came when I was invited to submit a photo to a museum exhibit alongside several noteworthy art photographers. It was an incredible honor, and I eagerly submitted a piece. But the experience was a stark reminder of how the art world operates—talent alone isn't enough. It's about connections, about knowing the right people who can open doors. Yet, those same doors can close just as quickly if you fall out of favor.

Reflecting now, while I had the passion and the eye for photography, I lacked the drive to navigate the social and business aspects of the art world. I wasn't willing to play the game that so many others did.

It reminds me of Harry Chapin's *Mr. Tanner*, a man who loved to sing and, after much encouragement, arranged to perform in New York City. The critics were harsh, and Mr. Tanner returned home, seeking the quiet solitude of his small shop, where he sang—not for fame or approval, but because it made him whole. And that was enough. Or perhaps I'm more like Vincent Van Gogh, whose unique style was dismissed by those who dictated the rules of art.

I find myself somewhere in between these two stories—an artist who struggled to find their place in a world that often values connections and conformity over genuine passion and vision. Maybe that's why I ended up where I am now—reflecting on a life that could have been, rather than one that was.

Those memories left me feeling somber. But I had to shake them off—I still needed to make arrangements for Mom's burial. As I reflected on my own struggles for understanding, I realized how much of it tied back to what I'd inherited from her and our family. The cold was starting to seep through my coat, so I returned to my rental car and drove to the funeral home.

The funeral home had handled so many of our family's funerals over the years. It was comforting to know that Mom would be taken care of by people familiar with our history, even if I didn't know them personally.

I was struck by their sensitivity as we went through the process of choosing a casket and making final arrangements. They showed me photographs of the different styles, and I remembered they had done Granny's funeral too. That made the decision easier—whatever my grandmother had, my mother would have too.

It felt good to have this part taken care of. When Mom's time came, it would be one less thing to worry about. As I left the funeral home, a humorous thought crossed my mind. They still had boxes of matches to give out—a rarity these days, with smoking so unpopular. I couldn't help but think it looked like a Do-It-Yourself cremation kit.

I got back to Mom's house around noon. For the next twenty-six hours, I sorted and cleaned, losing track of time. I never imagined how much work it would take to close down a home. Every box I went through held memories— not just of her, but of her life with my father. The hopes and dreams she'd had for us children, and the ones they had shared together before everything changed.

Many of those dreams seemed to have ended with the divorce. Yet, somehow, she had saved all the gifts and notes we gave her over the years. It stirred up so many memories, adding to the melancholy of the situation. And I still couldn't contact anyone—if my brothers found out, it would cause an uproar. I pushed through, getting just enough sleep to keep going until it was time to head to the airport on Sunday.

* * *

The rush of air streaming over the plane as it headed westward helped to quiet the weekend. I turned off my light and lifted the shade to peer out. It was a clear night. Off in the distance, the darkness abruptly ended where the waters of Lake Michigan met the bright city lights of Chicago.

I could see ribbons of orange and blue-white lights tracing the roads, weaving through the landscape like veins of energy. How we've covered our little planet.

I watched the lights fade away as we flew pass the city, slowly giving way to the empty darkness of rural Illinois. I took in the view until the last glimmers disappeared, then sat back and relaxed for the rest of the flight.

What Remains

Boston

For the two years Mom lived in Boston, I made it a point to visit her at least once a quarter. Those trips felt like a small escape from my own chaotic life, offering me the chance to step into hers, even briefly. Flying across the country gave me plenty of time to think—or perhaps it was the quiet, open skies that allowed my thoughts to drift away entirely, giving me the mental pause I needed.

With the four-hour flight, two-hour time difference, baggage claim, rental car pickup, and the hour-long drive, I usually arrived around 2:00 a.m.. Exhausted as I was, by breakfast Mom's joy of seeing me made every moment of the trip worth it. Who wouldn't do that?

I'd often try to coax her into a bit of light gardening—something she had once loved—but even that simple joy was slipping away from her. Still, those moments, however fleeting, felt like holding on to pieces of who she was.

We were fortunate to have met a very kind care manager named Sally. Of the three or four managers Mom had over those years, Sally was by far the best. She often reminded me, *"You need to live in the moment. It's your mother's world now. She only has the moment, and then it's gone. She may never be able to recall it again."*

Those words stuck with me, though living them wasn't easy.

It was hard for me to stay present, to anchor myself in the current moment with Mom. I couldn't rely on shared memories of the past—they were often lost to her. Nor could I plan for a future she might never understand. But in a way, this gave me permission to set aside the burdens of my own life, even if just temporarily. When I was with Mom, that was all I needed to focus on. Being present became a gift I could give her and, in turn, a gift I gave myself.

Sally's wisdom extended beyond living in the moment. She also encouraged me to think about Mom's quality of life. It wasn't just about keeping her safe or meeting her basic needs; it was about asking hard questions: Is life truly meant to be confined to the walls of a dementia ward? The question haunted me, especially as I saw the reality of nursing homes—places where low-paid staff, overworked and underappreciated, sometimes took out their frustrations on those most vulnerable.

I saw the results of this vulnerability starkly one day during a visit. By this time, Mom was living at an assisted living facility in Denver. The facility had wonderful, bright gardens that reminded me of the ones she had lovingly tended at her home. But that day, Mom was unusually quiet, her hands resting in her lap, one covering the other as if guarding a secret. Something about her stillness unsettled me. Her face carried an expression I couldn't quite place—sadness, confusion, or perhaps loss, all swirling together in her dementia world.

Gently, I coaxed her to show me what she was hiding. Slowly, she uncovered her hand. I froze, staring at the bruises on her fragile skin and the empty space where her prized large star sapphire ring should have been.

A wave of emotions hit me—anger, sorrow, helplessness. I didn't see what had happened, but the bruises told the story. Someone had taken the ring, likely prying it off her hand, leaving marks that were more than skin deep.

It was a painful reminder of how defenseless Mom had become, completely reliant on others for her safety and dignity. Dementia had already stripped away so much—her independence, her ability to express herself fully—and now it exposed her to a world where even small treasures could be stolen, ripped from her hand without care or remorse.

That moment reshaped how I saw caregiving. It wasn't just about managing her care or ensuring she was physically safe. It was about understanding her profound vulnerability, about advocating for her when she couldn't, and about seeing beyond the clinical tasks to the heart of what it means to truly care for someone.

Occasionally, she would surprise me with a glimmer of her old self. During the throes of my divorce, one summer evening, as we sat in the garden courtyard of the dementia ward, she turned to me and said, "Jim, you don't seem too happy. How's your life?"

The unexpected clarity in her voice caught me off guard. Part of me wanted to say, "Hi Mom, glad to have you back," but I was afraid she'd slip away as soon as I acknowledged it.

Instead, I sat there, unsure how to respond. I couldn't tell her how rough my divorce was or that my work was being relocated. As I answered, I couldn't help but think how kind she was in that moment, whether she realized it or not. It made her dementia all the more heartbreaking.

Sally was right—life is made up of fleeting moments that form our memories. Without those memories, how do we know we truly exist? We share our lives through shared memories, revisiting the past together. But for Mom, those memories had already slipped away.

When my sister moved away from Boston around the time Mom's house was sold, we had to make a difficult decision. We decided Mom should stay in Boston because most dementia wards wouldn't allow her to keep her thirteen-year-old miniature poodle, Megan. The two of them were inseparable.

But in October of that year, Megan stopped eating and drinking, spending all day curled up in her bed. I knew what was happening. The vet had discovered a tumor in Megan's stomach the previous year, but she was too old for surgery. I arranged for the facility manager to accompany Mom to the vet. It was a terribly sad day— Mom, alone in her world of dementia, losing the only living being she still felt close to.

It took Mom about a week to accept Megan's death, but this loss created an opportunity for her to move closer to family again. I became the next logical person for her to live nearby. By mid-December, I had found a facility in Denver that I thought she would like, one with a park-like setting that seemed her style. On December 20th, I flew to Boston to bring her to Denver.

The flight back was full of unknowns. I wasn't sure what unexpected events might arise, given how severe Mom's dementia had become. While she could still handle basic tasks like going to the bathroom independently, her trust in me to navigate unfamiliar situations was evident. Still, things didn't always go smoothly.

At the security checkpoint, my carefully rehearsed plan fell apart. As I was placing my items in the bin, a TSA agent motioned for Mom to walk through the metal detector — still wearing her shoes. My heart raced as the alarm blared. I rushed to the other side, only to see the agent preparing to wand and frisk Mom.

It was almost comical, but Mom was having none of it. She had no idea what was happening and wasn't about to let a stranger touch her. Flustered and raising holy hell, she made quite the scene. I explained that she had dementia and asked if there was an alternative. But this was Boston's Logan Airport, known for its heightened security in the years following 9/11. The agent refused to budge.

After several tense minutes and a discussion with higher-ups, they finally allowed her to go back through the metal detector without her shoes. Thankfully, this time, there were no alarms. I was immensely relieved that the culprit had been her shoes and not the underwire in her bra.

The flight itself turned out to be pleasant. I had enough miles to upgrade us to First Class, and the larger seats provided much-needed comfort and privacy. The extra space made a world of difference, and I couldn't imagine how difficult it would have been in coach.

As we flew west, sparkles of light began to dance around us, catching my eye. The effect was almost ethereal — comforting yet too tangible to be purely a spiritual sign. After a moment, I realized the sunlight streaming through the window was reflecting off Mom's diamond ring. I acknowledged the moment as fitting and welcomed it.

She wore two rings: her wedding set on her right hand and a stunning dark blue star sapphire on her left, both now impossible to remove due to the swelling in her hands. The diamonds caught the light, scattering shimmering patterns around us. I watched the sparkles, feeling an unexpected sense of peace, as if this small display of beauty was meant just for us. It was a memory that, for now, only one of us could hold onto.

Over the years, Mom had developed a strong attachment to me. She would often ask what I was having for dinner and then order the same. She even bought the same car I did. While this behavior sometimes annoyed me, it could also feel unsettling, almost inappropriate.

Her dementia made these feelings worse, as it often blurred the boundaries between our relationship roles. She knew I was a male figure in her life, but sometimes she couldn't remember if I was her son, her boyfriend, or even her husband.

During our flight to Denver, she occasionally thought I was her husband, believing I was bringing her to my home. I understood that this confusion was common in dementia, but it was still deeply unsettling. I did whatever I could to keep her calm, even if it meant playing along, but it left me feeling emotionally drained.

Moving to Denver wasn't just a transition for her—it was one for me, too. Being closer meant I could visit more often, at least every other week. But during the nearly two years she lived there, I sometimes had to cut visits short when her confusion became overwhelming. It saddened me, but I knew I had to protect my own well-being.

Boston had been another chapter in her life, one that had now closed. Denver was a new beginning for both of us, but I couldn't shake the feeling that time was slipping away, that no matter where she lived, some things were beyond my control.

Unlike in Boston, where we had others managing her care, Denver required me to take a more active role—buying her necessities, handling appointments, and negotiating her care. At times, it felt like a full-time job. I did my best to balance her needs while holding onto some sense of normalcy in my own life, but deep down, I knew the move wouldn't change the inevitable.

Finally, Answers

It was around this time, with frequent flights between Denver, Cleveland, and Boston, that I found myself reflecting deeply during those long hours in transit. The ever-shifting patterns of clouds and the vast landscapes far below seemed to mirror the questions swirling in my mind. Flying gave me space—both literal and metaphorical—to think, to question, and to start piecing together some long-sought answers about myself.

When I wasn't in the air, my daily hour-long drives to work became another outlet for introspection. Audiobooks turned those drives into opportunities to explore new ideas, each trip to the library a chance to find something that might spark curiosity or understanding.

Occasionally, I stumbled upon a book by sheer accident—something I hadn't planned on but that turned out to be captivating. Other times, I got reading ideas from radio shows where authors were interviewed, and book reviews shared.

One particular recommendation stood out. I heard a review of *An Anthropologist on Mars* by Oliver Sacks, and something about it struck a chord with me. Reading Sacks' accounts of people navigating unique neurological conditions led me down a path of deeper exploration.

That's when I discovered *Unwritten Rules of Social Relationships* by Temple Grandin and Sean Barron. The title alone resonated with me, as if it held the key to everything I felt I had missed or struggled to understand my whole life.

I wasn't expecting much—just another take on a world that had never made sense to me. But as I flipped through the pages, something shifted. The words weren't describing *other* people. They were describing *me*.

As I devoured the book, I found myself identifying with so many of the traits and experiences described. It was as if someone had finally put words to the silent struggles I had carried for years. Suddenly, various memories and comments came rushing back.

I remembered the Head Master at boarding school remarking that I didn't seem to make many friends, a comment that puzzled me then but now made perfect sense. I thought about the countless moments when conversations moved too fast, when I missed the cues that others seemed to pick up effortlessly. All those years of feeling like I was watching life from behind glass, of trying to mimic what came naturally to everyone else—there was a reason for it. A framework. A name.

Autism.

The word sat there, clear and undeniable. It wasn't an excuse. It wasn't an escape. It was the corner piece of a puzzle I'd spent my whole life trying to put together. And now, finally, the picture was coming into focus.

I thought about the ease with which I learned visually, even when reading was a struggle due to my dyslexia, and how that might have been a sign of my brain compensating in ways typical for someone on the spectrum. And then there was the fact that I had been late to begin speaking, another classic clue I had never fully connected.

It was in this moment of reflection that another thought crystallized: For most of my life, I had assumed that my sense of isolation—the feeling of being on the outside looking in—was due to my dyslexia and how it affected my interactions with others. But now, I realized it wasn't just the dyslexia. The isolation ran deeper.

It was about being on the autism spectrum. This revelation shifted my understanding of myself entirely. What I had once attributed to learning difficulties was, in fact, a part of a broader and more complex picture of how my brain worked and how I navigated the world.

Based on all these insights and how much I related to the experiences described in Grandin and Barron's book, I concluded that autism defined who I was. It explained so much of my life, from my social difficulties to my unique ways of processing information.

A memory of my mom's casual remark surfaced then: how doctors had once suspected I was autistic but decided I was too high functioning. I realized that this definition—high-functioning autism—fit me perfectly.

Eager to validate this new understanding, I consulted with a psychologist. They listened as I shared my discoveries and experiences and, after some discussion and assessment, confirmed my suspicions. That moment was a turning point. Everything began to make sense, as if the pieces of a lifelong puzzle were finally coming together.

Finally, I had a name—a condition that explained me, explained my being. But having a label was just the beginning of a much longer journey toward understanding. For the rest of my life, and certainly over the next 20 years, I slowly began to wake up to all the ways autism had shaped and continues to shape my experiences. It was a gradual realization, unfolding layer by layer as I connected more dots between the past and present.

I can't claim to undo a life that was molded by autism. The patterns, the ways I adapted (or struggled to adapt), were deeply ingrained, sculpted by years of navigating a world that often didn't make sense to me.

But at least now I had a working explanation—a framework for understanding my quirks, my social missteps, and the unique lens through which I see the world. There was no cure, no way to limit or change the way autism manifests in me. And honestly, this is who I am.

Coming to terms with this wasn't easy. Waking up to the full weight of my struggles, without the buffer of distraction, often felt overwhelming. Work was my saving grace, offering a steady rhythm and a sense of purpose that kept me grounded. It wasn't just about earning a paycheck; it gave me a way to stay connected to a world that might otherwise feel distant. For someone like me, living with autism, structured routines and predictable tasks were invaluable. They provided stability when everything else felt uncertain.

But when the pandemic forced me into early retirement, that stability disappeared. With no work to keep me distracted, the sheer weight of knowing, understanding, and realizing how autism had shaped my life and decisions became unavoidable. My days felt consumed by regrets, spilling over and leaving me searching for ways to quiet those thoughts.

It was a harsh reality—one I hadn't anticipated but could no longer ignore. Yet, amidst that harshness, the language I had gained through my diagnosis became an anchor. It allowed me to reframe my struggles as part of a bigger story, not just a list of regrets but a journey toward understanding and acceptance.

I can only hope that those who knew me—friends, family, acquaintances-might find it in their hearts to excuse the awkwardness, the misunderstandings, or the times I missed social cues. I hope they can forgive me if my behavior ever strained or fractured our relationship.

This diagnosis didn't fix everything, but it gave me the language to understand myself better. More than that, it brought a measure of peace, knowing that my struggles had always been part of a bigger story.

Perhaps I never fully woke up to all the ways autism shaped me — and maybe that's for the best. Staying engaged in the structured world of work allowed me to find comfort and peace, even when the rest of life sometimes felt just out of reach.

Outlook on Life

For the next two years, life settled into a quieter rhythm. Mom's health in Denver remained stable, aside from the gradual decline typical of dementia. The hostility between my siblings eased — perhaps because, once the house was sold and the family belongings were divided, there was nothing left to fight over. It was a welcome reprieve after years of dealing with Mom's illness and being the target of my siblings' darker sides.

I often joked that I now truly understood why friends and family are two different groups. Family might not qualify as friends, but good friends could certainly make up for it. I realized that during my mother's decline, the only times my siblings acted friendly were when they needed something from me. Once they got what they wanted, I was on my own.

The media, especially TV, profoundly influenced how I understood relationships and the world. The idealized families like The Brady Bunch or Leave It to Beaver seemed worlds away from my reality. Yet, I also saw flawed characters on screen, grappling with their own struggles to connect amidst the selfishness and egotism around them. Their stories resonated with me, reflecting my own challenges in navigating relationships and feeling understood. Perhaps this is why I found comfort in stories that mirrored my own sense of being misunderstood.

One pivotal moment came when I was six or seven, watching Gigot, a film about a kind-hearted, mute janitor. I identified so deeply with the character that I cried myself to sleep, sensing a future where others wouldn't understand me. Later, movies like Jonathan Livingston Seagull and books like Illusions by Richard Bach solidified this sense of being an outcast, yet also inspired me to rise above my limitations.

Jonathan Livingston Seagull was never just about a bird—it was about breaking free and forging your own path, a struggle I knew well. The story paralleled my struggles with dyslexia and the public school system, which had underestimated me. I knew I was intelligent, but reading and writing never came easily. When a psychologist once said I had a "superior ability to express myself," the irony wasn't lost on me—I couldn't even spell.

Books like Illusions and Inner Skiing offered me a new perspective on life. They taught me the power of simply being—of awareness without overthinking. In Steamboat, I tested these principles, embracing my own adventure beyond what anyone expected of me.

Yes, I faced struggles, but I didn't let them define me. Instead, I chose to live consciously, aware of my challenges but not consumed by them. For a while, I believed I had found balance. But as life often does, it had more lessons waiting for me—ones that would test everything I thought I had learned.

Hitting Rock Bottom and Fighting Back

My life was collapsing. At 46, I was drowning under pressures I couldn't escape. The company that had acquired my workplace was dismantling it piece by piece, leaving my job in turmoil, with no guarantee of how long I'd remain employed. The divorce settlement demanded much more than I had. My mother's care rested entirely on me, and my brother's relentless legal threats only added to the weight. Everything felt like it was spiraling out of control.

One day, in a moment of desperation, I went to a gun shop and found myself staring at the pistols on display. Through the glass, I watched people practicing at the indoor range, each shot hitting the target. I knew what I was contemplating. The realization frightened me, and I immediately left. That night, I wrote in my journal:

I look into the mirror, my eyelids half-opened, cutting across the top of my pupils. Through half-open eyes, I look at life. The heaviness that has weighed on my eyelids has also pulled down the corners of my mouth. The smile I once had for the world has become inverted. I wouldn't feel so bad if I had spent the night drinking or drugging. But it is only living that has done this.

I continued writing, letting my thoughts spiral into darker places. What would it feel like if I had reached the end?

The steel was colder than I had imagined. I could taste the powder that had exploded inside the barrel at the range earlier in the day. Soon, the steel warmed around my lips, and the powder began to taste like a very charbroiled steak. I sat there. How odd it was, the end just a click away.

Even in this imagined scenario, something stirred in me. My cheek felt moist. I brushed my hand across my face and saw the droplet on my fingertips. The months of crying and wailing in my mind faded into silence. Calmness entered the room.

Then, like an alarm sounding from deep within, the question shot up—How had I let myself get to this point?

I sat there, suddenly clear-minded.

Enough!

I put down the pen. Something inside me knew I had hit rock bottom without being buried. I knew what I had to do. I cursed, again and again, but then I began searching for ways to pull myself out of this pit.

I went to my five-by-ten-foot storage locker and took photos of everything inside. I liked everything in there, but the weight of my life was too heavy to carry any longer. It was time to let go. With eBay in its infancy, I discovered a new way to let go—one sale at a time, one less burden to carry.

Over the next nine months, I sold everything in storage and paid off the court-ordered divorce settlement. But I was on a roll, and it felt freeing. I turned to the items in my apartment next. I didn't fully understand what I was doing, but I knew it felt right. Within a year, I was down to the essentials: a bed, the desk Grandpa gave me, clothes, a computer, and a few other items.

Shedding my own past felt liberating. But I had no idea that soon, I'd be unearthing another life—one filled with secrets I never saw coming.

Mother's Hidden Struggles

While cleaning out my own belongings, vowing never to let my life accumulate the kind of clutter I found at Mom's house, I came across the things I had saved of hers. Most of it was legal papers, some trinkets, and old letters. But then, tucked among the mundane, I found her charm bracelet—a piece of jewelry she had loved wearing when we were children.

I could still see it in my mind, dangling from her wrist, its charms catching the light and drawing my gaze. It was a jumble of tiny objects—sharp and hard when you looked closely, but together, they seemed soft, almost comforting. I'd ask her, more than once, to tell me about them.

She would smile, gently twisting the bracelet around her wrist as she spoke.

"This plane reminds me of when I flew with my father. And these baby shoes are for you and your brothers and sister. You're my love and joy."

I could see it all now. The steel drum charm had to be from her trip to Barbados with her parents, a story she loved to tell. She talked about the fun they'd had, even seeing the Queen of England. Mom always brought us souvenirs from her trips, though I think she regretted bringing home a real steel drum when our overenthusiastic playing tested her nerves.

There were bowling charms—Mom had loved to bowl, as many did in the '50s and early '60s. A banjo and a bullfighter, mysteries I never solved, perhaps tied to some other adventure. College and school charms, and a calendar marking the shared birth date of her and her father. They, at least, had that in common.

But the charm that always drew me in was the mustard seed. Encased in a clear dome, it seemed to hold light within itself, like a tiny eye watching the world.

Mom would say, "This is a mustard seed. Though it's very small, it grows into a very large plant. Remember, honey, great things often start from small beginnings."

Holding the bracelet, I felt connected to the mother I knew. But as I dug deeper, I uncovered something that made me question how well I had really known her. As I sifted through another box, I uncovered her old purses. Inside one, tucked away in a hidden pocket, was a small pillbox—blue with intricate gold outlines. It was beautiful, almost delicate. I opened it and found two quarters of a blue pill and a third white pill.

The realization hit me immediately. After my sister and I took over Mom's healthcare from my older brother, she had warned me about Mom's Valium use. We'd tracked down pharmacy records from several drugstores near her house, revealing a 90-day supply of Valium refilled like clockwork.

Holding the pillbox, it all fell into place. This was the final puzzle piece: Mom had been a socially acceptable drug addict. The polished, graceful woman I knew had relied on Valium to navigate her world. The first clue had been the pharmacy records; the second was a letter I found she had written to Dad during her freshman year in 1950.

"I know you don't like me smoking," she wrote. "It's a bad habit, but it helps to calm me. College is very stressful... Mom gave me one of her little pills when things are just too much to handle."

Granny must have used sedatives too. It explained so much—why Mom never drank (she knew better than to mix alcohol with Valium) and why her occasional fits of anger seemed so sudden and intense.

During my third and final attempt at college, my advisor had studied the effects of Valium on aggressive behavior, concluding that it heightened aggression. It all made sense now.

She had always carried herself with poise, but beneath that, she was a woman who needed reassurance—a kind word, a sense of belonging. Maybe that's why she clung to the little blue pills. They didn't just calm her nerves; they helped her feel steady in a world that often left her uncertain.

The debutante whose name had appeared in the social registries wasn't addicted to cocaine or heroin but to the little blue pill prescribed by countless psychiatrists in the 20th century. The same pill that promised to calm the nerves of a generation had become her crutch.

Even after our parents are gone, we keep uncovering pieces of them—some bring comfort, others change everything we thought we knew. We forget that they, too, are human—fallible, fragile, and struggling in ways we often don't see. They lived through tough times, just as we do. And in those struggles, they carried secrets we only stumble upon by chance—long after they're gone.

Final Chapter

The final week of Mom's life began the way so many moments in this journey had—without warning and a phone call. This time, it came mid-Monday morning.

"Hello, Jim," Erin, our Care Manager, said. "Your mother became very ill yesterday. She vomited, and it was bright green. She hasn't eaten since yesterday morning. Can you go over and check on her?"

"Sure," I replied, trying to mask the concern in my voice. The familiar mix of worry and duty settled in as I headed to her room.

When I arrived, I found Mom curled up in a tight ball, more vulnerable than I'd ever seen her. The sight was startling. *Oh, Mom, I thought, what have you gotten yourself into this time?* I softly called her name.

"Mom."

No movement.

"Mom."

Still nothing.

Her room, normally so tidy, bore the signs of neglect—small indicators that she'd been in bed since the day before. A green stain on the floor caught my eye, and without thinking, I covered it with a hand towel, a reflex born of habit.

A floor attendant came in.

"We tried to get her to breakfast but she just refused. We can't force her," she said.

Next the morning shift nurse came in, probably having heard I was there.

"Morning, Jim. Glad you're here. She didn't want any food yesterday. She wouldn't budge from her bed."

I wasn't sure what to do. Would moving her make a difference? Still, she needed more care.

"Can you move her to the nursing ward for more medical care?" I asked.

"It's not that easy. They're full, and even if a bed opens up, there's only so much they can do. They probably can stabilize her, maybe start an IV until you can arrange a room at the hospital."

Hospital? I thought. No—Mom had endured enough. Needles, procedures, strangers making choices for her. A hospital would prolong things, not heal them. It would keep her body going, but it wouldn't see her, wouldn't honor the person she was. If this was the end, she should be where she felt safest—in her own bed.

"Ok, please see if there is a bed and get an IV going. I'll come back after work."

Before leaving I went back to check on her one last time before leaving. She stirred slightly, opening her eyes when I called her name. She recognized me, but there was no reaction—no smile, no acknowledgment. This was so unlike her.

I could not concentrate at work. My mind was full of worry. I began to mull over what I would say to my siblings. I hadn't talked with any of them in a long while.

I returned to the nursing ward around 5:00.

"How's my mother?"

"Yes, hi. We tried to administer the IV, but she fought us. We can't restrain her, force it on her. That's something a hospital would have to do."

"What about a mild sedative?"

The nurse hesitated. "We can try, but there are no guarantees."

A more senior nurse came by. "Jim, everything is pointing to sepsis."

"What's that?"

"It's like a virus in the blood—people like your mom rarely recover. You'd have to admit her to a hospital, and maybe they could treat it. But with her dementia as severe as it is, even if they cured the infection, the dementia would likely get much worse."

I'm stunned. *Wow.*

I had made a call to my sister, hoping that I would have her to help go through this. But no answer. The decisions were all on me.

The head nurse spoke gently. "You should think about the quality of life. . . . I'm sorry."

"We can call hospice for you," she continued. "They're close by and experienced in these situations."

I went back to Mom's room and stood by her bedside one last time before leaving for the night, her room dark and quiet, with the occasional voices out in the hall.

As I stood there, my mind raced ahead to what I would say to my siblings. How would they take the news? Would they even respond?

Or would this, once again, turn into an attack—more criticism about how I was handling Mom's care?

None of them truly understood the weight of what they had left me to carry. They got to sit at a distance, free from the daily pressures of keeping things legal, above board, and as smooth as possible. I had spent years balancing their demands, trying to keep the peace, making sure everything was done right—something they never had to worry about.

"Get some rest, Mom," I whispered before stepping out.

I could only leave messages on my sister's phone but was able to reach my brothers to alert them to this latest downturn before I called it a day.

I woke early and drove through the light snowfall to visit her. Everything still felt unreal. The past 24 hours had been filled with impossible decisions—sepsis, no IV, hospice. My siblings still weren't stepping up, and I was carrying this alone. Had I done the right thing? Had I made the right calls?

The snow blanketed everything in a hushed, motionless, serene white—nothing like what I was about to walk into. As I got out of the car, a thought crossed my mind: If this was the week, Mom had chosen a beautiful time to die.

Inside, the nursing ward buzzed with activity, a sharp contrast to the stillness outside. Despite the previous day's conversations, nothing had changed. The nurses still couldn't administer the IV. When I entered her room, she was awake, no longer curled up, but still hadn't eaten or drunk anything—day two without sustenance.

My younger brother called while I was there, and I held the phone to Mom's ear, his voice reaching out to her in a way only a son can. She smiled—a small, significant reaction but one that told me she was still in there, somewhere amidst the fog of dementia.

I left for work, my thoughts consumed by her fragile state.

By noon, I couldn't focus and returned to check on her. The nurses told me Mom couldn't stay in the nursing unit much longer—it was either the hospital or back to her room. The hospital would only keep the body functioning, not let her live.

I knew in my heart that wasn't what she wanted. Still, saying the words—call hospice—felt like crossing an invisible line, one I wasn't ready for. But there was no other choice.

The hospice team arrived; their compassion was evident, even through my numbness. They explained what would happen next, offering comfort I was too overwhelmed to feel. When they assessed Mom, they also determined she had sepsis. Gently, they informed me that she likely had less than 72 hours.

The realization hit hard—this was it, the final chapter of her life.

In moments like this, families rarely say it out loud, but they know. There's no more fighting—just waiting. Hoping the end comes gently. Some even find themselves wishing for something final—pneumonia, sepsis, or another complication—anything that would bring release without prolonging the suffering.

For Mom, it was sepsis. Untreatable. Even if it weren't, the infection would have only worsened her dementia, pulling her even further into the abyss of lost memories. The doctors knew it. Eventually, I had to accept it too.

Easing her way out was the last, and only, thing I could do for her.

Wednesday, Mom was back in her room. She stayed curled up in bed. A hospice nurse and spiritual advisor was assigned to us.

"Hi, I'm Rebeca from Hospice. This is a very challenging time in life. I want you to know we not only care for people like your Mom, but we are here for you too. . . . Are you religious?"

I shook my head. "No, more spiritual if anything."

"Well, I'm here if you'd like to say a little prayer, . . . or have a quiet moment . . . ."

"Thanks." But I knew this was too much, and I was focused on making sure I covered all the bases, before even thinking about it. Sometimes, it's easier to keep moving, to focus on the next step rather than stop and feel. If you let it in too soon, you might not get through it.

I was still making calls to my sister. *Why hadn't she responded to the many voice messages I left?* Damn, was she going to leave me to handle this by myself?

Thursday, when I opened Mom's door, I found my sister and Rebeca.

Of course, she shows up at the last minute.

I figured she couldn't handle it, avoiding it as long as possible. But later, as we sat composing Mom's obituary, she told me, "Mom said she was there when Granny died—to see her final breath."

Maybe that's why she came now—to be there for Mom's, too.

"Sorry—I was on a trip and didn't get your messages until yesterday. I drove the five hours to get here and arrived after midnight. I just stayed here on the floor with Mom."

I exhaled. "I'm so glad you're here." And I meant it

"Rebeca was catching me up on things."

Thursday felt like the final gift Mom gave us—her presence, her love, her eyes full of warmth as she ate for the first time since this all began.

She sat up in bed, my sister and I on either side of her, the three of us forming a small, intimate circle—like some unspoken ritual we didn't realize we had been waiting for. My sister gently lifted a spoonful of Jello to Mom's lips, completing the quiet, inevitable cycle—mother caring for daughter, now daughter caring for mother. Mom accepted it, savoring the taste as if it were her first time. Each sip of soup brought her a quiet joy, her gaze shifting between us as if she wanted to take us in, to remember us as much as we would remember her. She nodded slightly after each bite—a silent acknowledgment, a moment of gratitude, carrying the weight of something unspoken but deeply understood.

The snow-covered garden outside her window reflected soft light into the room, casting a gentle glow over everything. The light caught in the lines of her face, in the curve of her smile, making the moment feel almost sacred. She was still in her dementia world, but there was no mistaking it—she knew where she was in life.

On Monday, I had heard her murmur something under her breath, almost to herself: "I've done it now." It was the closest she had come to acknowledging her sickness, to recognizing what lay ahead.

And yet, in this moment, there was no fear. No sadness. Just this quiet, simple joy.

For a while, we talked—small memories, easy stories. We let the past drift between us, pulling warmth from the Christmases that had come before. I reminded her how she used to stay up late on Christmas Eve, making sure every little detail was just right—the crèche scenes arranged with care, tiny snow-covered pine trees in the windows, the gifts placed perfectly under the tree. My sister laughed, adding how she always made us wait just a little longer before finally letting us down the stairs to tear into our presents.

Mom listened, nodding, a soft smile playing at her lips. Maybe she was remembering, maybe not—but it didn't matter. The feeling was there.

For a fleeting moment, it felt like those Christmas mornings again—when we were small, when everything was warm and safe, when we believed there would always be another holiday, another gathering, another moment like this.

But I knew this one was different.

This was the last gift she could give.

As the hours passed, her energy waned.

By Friday, the change was undeniable. Her breaths were shallow, her once-bright eyes distant. My sister and I sat with her, speaking in hushed tones as the hospice nurse checked in periodically. The weight of the inevitable hung in the air, pressing down on every word and every silence.

I held Mom's hand—that same hand that had comforted me as a child. I wanted to say something profound, something to ease the passing for both of us, but no words came. Instead, I sat there, listening to the rhythm of her breathing, trying to memorize the moment while dreading its end.

Eventually, the heaviness became too much. I stood, kissed her forehead, and whispered, "I'll be back soon." Then I left, stepping out into the crisp winter air, seeking a moment to collect myself.

When the call came, I rushed back to be at her side, but it was too late.

Mom had died.

For a long moment, I just stood there. The room that had been hers for the last two years now felt empty—a silence so heavy, it pressed into my chest. My eyes landed on a photo pinned to her picture board, full of life and spirit. In that moment, I understood—her spirit, captured in that photograph, was still very much alive.

The logistics of death move fast. My prearrangements kicked in immediately. Within hours, her body was taken away, prepared for transport back to Cleveland, where she would be buried alongside her mother.

It was surreal—one moment, she was here, and the next, everything was already in motion to lay her to rest. I had expected this, planned for it, but the finality of it still hit hard.

That night, I woke around 1:00 AM with the uncanny awareness that Mom was leaning over my bed, just as she had when I was a child. Her presence was so strong, almost tangible. I felt her kind eyes, her gentle smile, as she said goodbye for the last time.

I whispered back, "Goodbye, thank you, I love you," and watched as she faded into the darkness.

The next morning, I returned to the facility to pack up her things. The snow from the night before had turned into a heavy, wet blanket, clinging to every tree branch and surface. As the sun rose, its intense light began to melt the snow, the sound of dripping water filling the air.

It felt like a cleansing—washing away the week's events, the final chapter in Mom's life.

On the flight back from her funeral, I reflected on everything that had happened over the past four years. Back home, while sorting through old papers, I stumbled upon my notebook from Steamboat. I flipped through its scattered thoughts until I landed on a page I hadn't noticed before—my epitaph, written at 21. At the top, I had scrawled, *Here it is.*

And there it was, summing up my life then—and perhaps still now.

> *As I continue my travels*
> *Seeing new and wonderful sights*
> *I often forget where I'm going*
> *It disturbs me to lose heading*
> *But one day I'll get there, I might*
> *Only to continue my travels.*

In Conclusion:

As I stand here now, reflecting on the words I wrote all those years ago, I see how my epitaph has come to define my life. The journey has never been a straight line. There have been times of confusion, of losing my way, but each experience has shaped me into who I am today.

Even now, I find myself standing at a threshold, ready to take the next step. I am ever traveling, discovering, and embracing the unknown. Death is the only destination we all share, and I'm not there yet.

Perhaps the greatest lesson is that life isn't about arriving at a destination—it's about continuing the journey, with all its unexpected twists and turns. As long as I'm here, I keep moving, keep searching, and keep discovering—whatever that may bring.

Epilogue

The COVID pandemic forced me into early retirement—something I hadn't prepared for. At first, I kept busy renovating condos, even flipping one at the peak of the market. Pure luck—just a week later, prices began to fall. But as the projects dwindled and I grew tired of remodeling work, I found myself with too much time on my hands and an unexpected visitor: nostalgia.

Fifteen years earlier, when I was fifty and my son was newly born, I had started writing a recounting of my life. Parenthood marked a fresh chapter, but it also made me reflect on the ones already written. That manuscript sat untouched for years, buried beneath daily distractions. Now, in the quiet of early retirement, it resurfaced. As I sifted through memories, I kept circling back to a time when life felt brighter—when I was doing exactly what I wanted: photography.

L.A. had an undeniable magic. Within 24 hours of arriving—without knowing a soul—I had a great job and a place to stay. That's almost unheard of. Looking back, it felt like I was meant to be there.

I worked on some of the best photographic images in Hollywood, rubbing elbows with renowned photographers. But slowly, the cracks began to show. The firehouse from *Emergency!* was just down the street from Dave's home in Sherman Oaks. The horse neighborhood from *Mr. Ed* was in Burbank, not far from where I lived. Everywhere I looked, I found echoes of the shows I grew up with.

Had the allure of L.A. been more about living inside a TV show than real life?

On one hand, L.A. was wearing on me—the dirt, the concrete, the relentless sprawl. Most of all, I struggled to connect with people who seemed superficial, always looking for an angle. The photo lab was my sanctuary. There, I belonged. Outside of it, things were different.

I had photographed an aspiring actress multiple times, but she never paid me. My only compensation was dinners with the producer who had introduced us, each one dangling the slim hope of connections that never materialized. And maybe they could have—if my goal had been to become a Hollywood photographer. But it wasn't. I just wanted to master color photography. That passion never grew beyond that.

And yet, another side of me saw the writing on the wall.

Computers were coming, and they were going to change everything. By the time I left L.A., the transition had already begun. The Hollywood lab I worked at merged with a retouching studio that had once relied on airbrushing. They invested over a million dollars in a digital system. When I visited in 1990, two short years after I left, I saw firsthand what the future looked like: a single person, in half a day, accomplishing what used to take a team of four several days to finish.

Years later, just before writing this book, I stumbled across an article from that retouching studio. The office manager detailed how digital photography had wiped out their entire business model—one that had sustained three generations of their family.

When I moved to Kent, everything changed. Small town. Open land. A sharp contrast to L.A., and I welcomed it. My photography flourished as I explored new ways to create images. I developed my *Northeast Ohio Series* and *Organic Series*, both of which caught the attention of Parker-Hannifin and Ernst & Young. *Organic* was a reaction against the razor-sharp, ultraprecise images I had spent four years producing in Hollywood. I turned to pinhole photography—true organic photography, where nothing artificial interfered with the light hitting the film.

After leaving L.A., the emotional decompression was brutal. I experienced moments of deep despair and, one night, a complete breakdown—gut-wrenching sobs, as though I were mourning the loss of a loved one.

But this was different.

It wasn't someone else I had lost; it was me.

Turning thirty was the start of it. At twenty-nine, the looming milestone filled me with dread. My peers had corporate jobs, homes, families. My life was a string of unstable gigs. Technology was creeping into photography, and the work I once loved was slipping away.

There's a line in *Moneyball* that sums it up well:
"Some get to play their childhood game, but one day, it will end."
For me, L.A. was that childhood game. And one day, it ended.

But L.A. isn't just about playing the game—it's about constantly reinventing it. Careers rise and fall overnight. Maybe I sensed that underneath it all. Maybe that's why I never saw myself as a Hollywood photographer. I wanted to master a craft, not chase a trend.

The question—*Why did I leave?*—surfaced when I had no projects to occupy my time. Had I been running all those years? It wasn't until I retired and ran out of ways to keep myself busy that I began to really confront it.

But as I wrote this book, another realization surfaced—one I hadn't fully grasped before.

I never thought of myself as isolated. Not really. I was just… me.

But in revisiting these moments, I see it now. Isolation wasn't just something I felt—it was something shaped by circumstance, by how the world saw me, by how I moved through it. Observing has always come naturally to me. Maybe that's why I was drawn to photography, to psychology, to stepping back and seeing patterns in the world around me.

School may have set me apart, but it also solidified what I do best— watch, analyze, understand. What began as forced separation became something else entirely: a way of engaging with the world, just from a different vantage point. And now, in retirement, what I've spent a lifetime seeing is what I leave behind.

And perhaps, by how my mother, who wrote for the local magazine, moved through it, too.

She was isolated in her own way, in ways I didn't recognize at the time. Maybe it was generational. Maybe it was just who we were.

And now, I wonder—how many of us live our lives without recognizing the patterns until much later? How many people only realize, in hindsight, what shaped them all along?

Life doesn't always take us where we expect to go. And yet, despite everything, I've come to understand that life is about navigating the uncharted waters, knowing that even when we lose our heading, we can still discover new and wonderful sights along the way.

As I leave these pages behind, my hope is that this journey of mine will resonate with yours—and that we all keep moving forward, even when the way is unclear.

www.ingramcontent.com/pod-product-compliance
Lightning Source LLC
Chambersburg PA
CBHW021102130626
46554CB00002B/483